"Dr. Wilson is an impactful preacher and first-rate professor who leverages these strengths in his latest gift to preachers, *Illustrating Well*. This book provided me with theological confidence and practical skill to communicate God's word with greater clarity and passion!"

—Zach Edwards,
senior pastor, Trinity Southern Baptist Church, Fresno, California

"Motivated by a love for God's word and the importance of preaching transformational sermons, Jim Wilson provides a fresh look at sermon illustrations and then helps the preacher craft them. Whether the preacher is writing his first sermon or his 500th, *Illustrating Well* will give him tools to effectively preach the Bible and see changed lives as people come to see God's truth in clear, easy to understand ways."

—Bryan Catherman,
pastor, Redeeming Life Church, Bountiful, Utah

"This is an amazing book. Jim Wilson writes from deep experience here, expounding with wisdom, thoughtfulness, and craftsmanship on the beauty of excellent sermon illustrations. It's all here, from the effective telling of classic stories to the careful construction of personal narratives. Wilson guides the reader to understand what their audience needs to hear and how the text needs to be engaged, always keeping the delivery of God's word as the prime focus. Remember those sermon illustration books on your shelves and computer? Throw them all away. Wilson's book is all you need to recognize, create, and deploy excellent, cogent, and powerful illustrations."

—Earl Waggoner,
r of biblical and theological studies,
Colorado Christian University

T0049523

"With godly wisdom, extensive research, over forty years of preaching, classroom experience teaching countless students, and a plethora of 'illustrations' and how they are categorized and used effectively or poorly, Dr. Jim Wilson passionately makes a compelling case for using illustrations well as we communicate God's word. Writing as he teaches, Dr. Wilson also draws the reader into an enriching journey at every turn, to inspire even seasoned communicators to stop and reevaluate our illustrations. Why? So our selected illustrations become helpers in transformative preaching and teaching. After all, the ultimate experience in Christian preaching and teaching is to be the Holy Spirit's sanctified vessels who present God's word such that people put their faith in Jesus and people grow as loyal followers of Jesus. *Illustrating Well* is an invaluable and must have resource for the classroom and for the personal libraries of serious communicators of God's precious word."

—Brian E. Kennedy,
senior pastor, Mt. Zion Church of Ontario;
associate professor of preaching, Gateway Seminary

"If you are looking for maximum impact in your preaching, *Illustrating Well* is the tool you need to get there. Dr. Wilson gives communicators a fresh look at delivering God's word with clarity and effectiveness. I highly recommend every pastor have this resource readily available to them."

—Josh Saefkow,
senior pastor, Flat Creek Baptist Church, Fayetteville, GA

"This is a book I will read every couple of years for the rest of my preaching career. *Illustrating Well* is another great tool for the preaching toolbox."

—Shawn Beaty,
senior pastor, Clovis Hills Community Church

"*Illustrating Well* is an accessible source of homiletical gold. From Wilson's careful encouragement to keep illustrations text-centered, to the many gems of practical and effective advice about constructing illustrations, this resource is a powerhouse for the preacher. Whether a seasoned pastor or a young preacher, anyone with the responsibility to communicate God's word will find *Illustrating Well* a worthy read and useful companion."

—Joe Slunaker,

assistant professor, California Baptist University

"After pastoring and sharing illustrations for thirty years, Jim's latest book was a much needed 'kick in the pants'! Jim helped me break out of my illustrating rut to be more engaging as I share God's word. As Jim reminds us, the illustrations we share should be more than interesting—they should create more interest in the text we are teaching. Rather than putting my illustrating on autopilot, Jim's research and practical insights helped me to curb my predictability and bring something new to how I illustrate my messages."

—Bob Johnson,

pastor, Grace Point Church, San Diego, CA

"There is an art to using illustrations effectively. Jim Wilson is one of the finest teachers I have ever known. He is likewise a gifted preacher of the gospel who takes us to school regarding one of the key factors in good preaching: the effective use of illustrations. You will be blessed and your communication strengthened by absorbing the rich instruction in *Illustrating Well*."

—J. Robert White,

president and CEO, Health Care Ministry Foundation

"Among great biblical preachers, often the skill that sets one apart from the others is their ability to effectively illustrate the biblical message. If preaching God's word is a craft, preachers should learn how to use every 'tool' in the preaching 'toolbox.' *Illustrating Well* enhanced my ability as a preacher to craft and properly utilize illustrations so that my hearers are more impacted by biblical truth."

—Jason Robertson,
lead pastor, Huntington Beach Church, CA

Illustrating Well

Preaching Sermons that Connect

Illustrating Well

Preaching Sermons that Connect

Jim L. Wilson

LEXHAM PRESS

Illustrating Well: Preaching Sermons that Connect

Copyright 2022 Jim L. Wilson

Lexham Press, 1313 Commercial St., Bellingham, WA 98225
LexhamPress.com

All rights reserved. You may use brief quotations from this resource in presentations, articles, and books. For all other uses, please write Lexham Press for permission. Email us at permissions@lexhampress.com.

Unless otherwise indicated, Scripture quotations are from the Christian Standard Bible, Copyright © 2017 by Holman Bible Publishers. Used by permission. Christian Standard Bible® and CSB® are federally registered trademarks of Holman Bible Publishers.

Scripture quotations marked (NASB) are from the New American Standard Bible®, Copyright 1960, 1962, 1963, 1968, 1971, 1972, 1973, 1975, 1977, 1995 by The Lockman Foundation. Used by permission.

Scripture quotations marked (NKJV) are from the New King James Version. Copyright 1982 by Thomas Nelson. Used by permission. All rights reserved.

Scripture quotations marked (NLT) are from the Holy Bible, New Living Translation, copyright © 1996, 2004, 2007, 2013 by Tyndale House Foundation. Used by permission of Tyndale House Publishers, Inc., Carol Stream, Illinois 60188. All rights reserved.

Print ISBN 9781683595892
Digital ISBN 9781683595908
Library of Congress Control Number 2021947099

Lexham Editorial Team: Elliot Ritzema, Andrew Sheffield, Allisyn Ma,
          Jessi Strong, Mandi Newell
Cover Design: Owen Craft, Brittany Schrock
Typesetting: Abigail Stocker

I dedicate this book to two colleagues,
Rodger Russell
and
Jim Sandell.
Both have worked with me for over a decade
in providing fresh sermon illustrations
to preachers around the world
at FreshMinistry.org.

Contents

Acknowledgments

Gateway Seminary

Thank you to the Board of Trustees of Gateway Seminary, President Jeff Iorg, and Academic Dean Michael Martin for the half-sabbatical leave to write this book.

Research Team

Thank you to Derick Wilson, my research assistant, for the hours he spent poring over books, journal articles, blogs, and sermons to bring pertinent quotes and examples to my attention.

Thank you to Doctor of Ministry candidates Leotra West and Joseph Douthitt, who conducted some preliminary research for this book as part of an independent study.

Influencers

Thank you to the following people, who offered their suggestions in response to questions I asked them about illustrating well or as they read drafts of the book.

- Dr. Randy Adams

- Dr. Greg Cole

- Ms. Jacqueline Garland

- Dr. Paul Kelly

- Dr. Deryl Lackey

- Rev. Min Lee

- Dr. Steven Lennertz

- Dr. Steve Long

- Dr. J. T. Reed

- Dr. Rodger Russell

Foreword

Paraphrasing Charles Spurgeon, sermon illustrations are the windows that let light into the message. They help clarify how biblical truth connects to life today. Jim Wilson has done an exceptional job in this book of teaching us how to do that more effectively.

Sadly, some preachers think sermon illustrations are extraneous to biblical preaching. They think declaring truth from the Bible means delivering a stiff monologue of biblical facts and theological propositions—perhaps sprinkled with biblical allusions or examples—with the unrealistic expectation that people will understand and apply what they are hearing. On the other extreme, some preachers think sermons are composed only of illustrations—cute or touching stories they string together in a moralistic manner to communicate some vague truisms (rather than Truth). Neither of these misguided methods gets the job done.

Good preaching is textually driven, taking the Bible seriously enough to use the text throughout the message. This kind of preaching exposes biblical truth but also applies it to contemporary hearers. Part of doing that well is using illustrations to drive home the point, deepen the impact, and make an emotional connection between the content and the hearer. Good illustrations create mental images that enable listeners to experience the text—seeing it played out in a concrete fashion or with an artistic flair.

Learning to illustrate well requires as much effort as learning to exposit Scripture. Most preachers understand the need to know at least some Greek and Hebrew, study the historical settings of biblical texts, delve into the cultural context surrounding eras of biblical history, and learn how to interpret different literary genres. They also understand the importance of both analyzing the meaning of a text and knowing how to interpret that meaning across the centuries from ancient cultures to current hearers. A similar effort is required to learn to illustrate well.

Good illustrating includes gathering material—a lot of material—to assure a steady supply of fresh illustrations. It includes knowing how to use various kinds of illustrations (less about your children would be a good start) and recognizing the settings where certain illustrations are most impactful (and knowing when to avoid using them). Good illustrating involves the discipline of using a wide variety of content based on your audience(s), the nature of the preaching event, and the text you are using.

I am enthusiastic about this book because my friend Jim Wilson is a good preacher. He is in front of a congregation almost every week, practicing what he teaches. His messages are always saturated with a biblical text, clearly applied to contemporary hearers, and brought to life with skillful illustrating. He is a model preacher who has trained countless others in the skills he has mastered. Fortunately, he has written those insights in books like this to help all of us who preach to do it better.

I am also grateful for this book because it extends Jim Wilson's teaching ministry. He is just as masterful in the classroom as in front of a congregation. It has been my pleasure to team teach with him on numerous occasions and I always learn something new. While you may not be able to sign up for his courses, the next best thing is reading his books on preaching. I commend this one to you, encourage you to read it carefully, and—more importantly—I ask you to put it into practice next Sunday when you stand to declare a word from God.

Jeff Iorg
President, Gateway Seminary

Introduction

Listeners, preachers, and homileticians generally agree that illustrations enhance sermons.[1] If used well, they help listeners understand, apply, or experience the text. However, to be effective, they must be used well. If not, they can get in the way of communicating the biblical message.

For instance, too many illustrations will dilute the sermon's substance.[2] Some personal illustrations can split the focus between the message and the messenger, drawing attention to the messenger instead of the message. Those that contain factual errors can destroy the preacher's credibility.

In short, if not used well, sermon illustrations can get in the way of the message instead of helping listeners understand, apply, or experience the text. However, when illustrations are used well, they break down communication obstacles.

---

1. There are some who dissent. For instance, Richard Farmer writes, "What sermon illustrations should be banned? Nearly all of them!" "What Sermon Illustrations Should Be Banned from Pulpits?," 31.

2. "One danger is to rely too much on stories. The one thing worse than a sermon without illustrations is a sermon that is nothing but illustrations; it is like the Empire State Building: 'one story on top of another.' All this does is present a sermon devoid of substance." Raiter, "On Sermons and Preaching," 95.

Communication: The Goal and
Some Obstacles to Reaching It

In communication, speakers attempt to replicate a message from their minds in the minds of their audience members. In the simplest of terms, transmitting meaning is the speaker's goal, while receiving meaning is the listener's goal. However, successful meaning transmission is not automatic—far from it. Public speaking is more like an NBA player attempting to dunk a basketball with two seven-foot players trying to block the shot than it is the layup line in a pregame warmup. While the obstacles speakers face are not as blatant as the basketball player's, they can be just as real and daunting.

One of the obstacles that get in the way of meaning transmission is that words have extrinsic meaning but no intrinsic meaning. Words simply carry meaning that the users will nuance or alter in the communication process. The way speakers deliver the words—the context, vocal inflections, facial expressions, and body language—is part of the meaning transmission. Some of those elements are under speakers' conscious control, but some of them are not, and likely, none of them is under their full control. Also, the listeners' level of concentration, their previous experience with the word, and other factors could nuance or alter the meaning.

Another obstacle is that a particular word may carry multiple meanings. "Apple" is not just a fruit. It can also refer to a computer or a watch. In some Latin American countries, "apple" (*manzana*) is also a term used to refer to a city block. While speakers can select a word to carry a specific meaning, the listeners might not experience a clean meaning transmission in the communication process, necessitating a feedback loop to ensure that the listeners are experiencing the meaning the speakers are intending.

Other obstacles, like miscommunication, the distance between people in a room, poor enunciation, unfamiliar accents, cultural differences, ambient noise, biases, and emotional dispositions, threaten pure meaning transmission and must be mitigated in appropriate ways by the speaker. In short, effective meaning transmission is not a slam dunk.

Additional Obstacles

In preaching, the goal is not exclusively to communicate the preacher's idea; it is to communicate the meaning that the biblical authors intended while they were under the inspiration of the Holy Spirit. This adds another layer of complication. The Bible is an ancient book written by multiple authors, each within the specific contexts of original audiences that spanned more than a thousand years. The geography, customs, culture, and languages of the Bible are foreign to most modern readers. All these realities form additional communication obstacles. This is where good sermon illustrations, used effectively, can help.

Sermon illustrations that are *familiar, clear, interesting,* and *appropriate* can assist audiences in understanding, applying, or experiencing the Bible's teachings. Good illustrations assist preachers in overcoming communication obstacles that hinder effective meaning transmission with their congregations.

Certainly, preachers have to get it right. Their sermons (including the illustrations) must be biblically accurate and theologically rigorous. However, good theology is not enough. Pastor and author J. D. Greear says, "I regularly look for both exegetical insight and illustrative insight as I'm researching specific texts, because the people in my church don't just need good theology; they need to understand and feel the gospel. And the perfect illustration or story will often make a gospel truth relevant in a way that dozens of word studies never will."[3]

---

3. Greear, "Pastor J.D., How Do You Prepare Your Sermons?"

The point is not that a well-illustrated sermon does not need theological rigor; nothing could be further from the truth. Every sermon should be theologically rich and thoroughly biblical and should have its meaning emerge from the text. Nevertheless, preachers should also present the message in a way that is accessible to people. Preaching professor James Cox writes:

> Many sermons fail, not because they are not based on sound exegesis, not because they are not arranged carefully or because they are not expressed precisely. They fail because preachers often take the people for granted. They use few or no examples to illustrate what they are talking about or to emphasize its reality, few or no comparisons to throw light on the subject.[4]

To reach the minds and hearts of their listeners, preachers must do more than explain truth; they must demonstrate how the truth relates to and works in real life. The truth must become more than an abstract concept; it must become a concrete reality—one that the listeners can relate to and apply to their lives. Seeing a concept demonstrated increases the hearers' understanding of the concept and their motivation to apply it to life situations.

There is something about a good illustration that helps the unfamiliar become familiar and the distant become close. In the Old and New Testaments, as well as throughout church history, prophets, teachers, and preachers have used illustrations to increase their effectiveness in communicating.

4. Cox, "Evaluating the Sermon," 230.

Truth Was Demonstrated
in the Old Testament

The Old Testament is filled with God's prophets demonstrating, not just proclaiming, God's message. When God wanted Jeremiah to understand the impending decay of Judah and Jerusalem, he had him buy a new linen loincloth and wear it without washing it. Later, God instructed Jeremiah to hide it for an extended period in the rocks next to the Euphrates River. After a long time, when God instructed him to, Jeremiah retrieved the rotten garment, which was now falling apart (Jer 13:1–8). After Jeremiah saw (and smelled) the result of the prolonged decay, he was prepared to fully hear and proclaim the message from God: "This is what the LORD says: Just like this I will ruin the great pride of both Judah and Jerusalem. These evil people, who refuse to listen to me, who follow the stubbornness of their own hearts, and who have followed other gods to serve and bow in worship—they will be like this underwear, of no use at all" (Jer 13:9–10).

This was not an isolated incident. On another occasion, God required the prophet Isaiah to walk around naked and barefoot for three years. Strange behavior, but it had a purpose—to illustrate that captivity was coming and that the people would walk into their destiny without anything (Isa 20:1–4). God also instructed one of his prophets to marry a prostitute, which became an analogy for Israel's unfaithfulness to God (Hos 1–3).

Sometimes God required his prophet to become the demonstration. Before Ezekiel lost his wife, God warned him that it was about to happen and instructed him not to go through traditional mourning rituals before the people. He could weep quietly, but not publicly, as was the custom of their times. He did as God instructed him. The morning after his wife passed away, the people came and asked him to explain why he was not mourning her:

So I answered them: "The word of the LORD came to me:
Say to the house of Israel, 'This is what the Lord GOD
says: I am about to desecrate my sanctuary, the pride of
your power, the delight of your eyes, and the desire of
your heart. Also, the sons and daughters you left behind
will fall by the sword. Then you will do just as I have
done: You will not cover your mustache or eat the bread
of mourners. Your turbans will remain on your heads and
your sandals on your feet. You will not lament or weep but
will waste away because of your iniquities and will groan
to one another.' " (Ezek 24:20–23)

The prophets helped the people understand, visualize, and
experience their message. They did more than tell the people
something; they demonstrated the truth.

Jesus used analogies to help people understand his teaching.
Jesus used normal, everyday items in people's lives to represent
extraordinary kingdom truths. John records many of these in his
Gospel. At a well, Jesus told a thirsty woman that he could provide "living water" that leads to eternal life (4:13). He spoke of
bread (6:35), light (9:5), doors (10:1–3, 9), and shepherds (10:11).
Beside the tomb of a dead man, he said that he is the resurrection and that those who believe in him will live even after they
die (11:25–26). He also taught using vines and branches (15:1–8),
servants and masters (15:20), a woman in labor (16:21), and lambs
(21:15–19). These analogies helped the people understand, apply,
and experience his message.

In the Sermon on the Mount in Matthew 5–7, Jesus used salt
(5:13), light (5:14), lamps and baskets (5:15), moths and rust (6:20),
birds (6:26), and flowers (6:28). He also used specks and planks
(7:3); dogs, pearls, and pigs (7:6); a hungry child (7:9); gates (7:13);
wolves (7:15); and grapes, bushes, trees, and fruit (7:16–20). Jesus

closed the sermon by referencing rain, floods, foundations, and buildings (7:24–27). Jesus used everyday, ordinary, familiar items from his hearers' lives to teach them something new—about a life that they could experience in his kingdom.[5]

Communicators Throughout Church History Used Illustrations

Augustine used illustrations "to draw people into this depth of Scripture."[6] The Dominicans compiled a collection of *exempla*—sermon illustrations—to provide examples of moral living.[7] Martin Luther worked to make biblical truth accessible to common people, and one of the ways he did that was with sermon illustrations.[8] He said that examples help listeners "understand more clearly and … remember more easily."[9]

However, this does not mean that preachers should use sermon illustrations with impunity or that all sermon illustrations

---

5. "The challenge of the Sermon is to proclaim and inform these two distinct dimensions: life in the present and eternal life in the future. Jesus responds to the challenge by giving his diverse audience pictures, stories, and illustrations to help his listeners see and understand the radical nature of this new reign." Fallon, "The Bible Preaches on the Bible," 298–99.

6. Sanlon, "Depth and Weight," 66.

7. "They also edited a number of biblical concordances to provide the preacher with effective texts. There were also collections of *exempla*, the medieval equivalent of sermon illustrations, taken from the lives of the saints and the moral lessons of daily life." Leonard, "Preaching in Historical Perspective," 28.

8. "Luther shows great realness, both in his personal grasp of Christian truth, and in his modes of presenting it. The conventional decorums he smashes, and with strong, rude, and sometimes even coarse expressions, with illustrations from almost every conceivable source, and with familiar address to the individual hearer, he brings the truth very close home. He gloried in being a preacher to the common people." Broadus, *Lectures on the History of Preaching*, 123.

9. Reinis, "*Exempla*," 284–85.

are created equal. Just as they can add to a sermon, they can also become a distraction. Instead of breaking down communication barriers, they can become an obstacle to meaning transmission. Besides, there are multiple types of illustrations, not all of them appropriate for every sermon or in every part of the sermon. This book will provide you with tools for evaluating sermon illustrations and guide you to use them well.

The Aim of This Book

The genesis of this book had two phases. The first was to search for a consensus among preachers and homileticians about what makes an effective sermon illustration. To this end, a team of researchers and I scoured over a hundred academic and popular preaching books that span over a hundred years; most of them are current, but others are from notable thinkers from earlier eras. We also searched through scholarly and popular journal articles and read reputable blogs. You will find quotes and references sprinkled throughout the book from this research. Some of the sources will be familiar to you, but others may not be. Some of the thinkers I cite are compatible with my conservative theological point of view, others are not.

To keep from breaking the flow, I've placed many of the quotations in the footnotes, not in the text. Some of the quotations provide a source that contributed to my current understanding, but others promote a roundtable conversation among them, you, and me. Certainly, my views will emerge, but my goal is not so much to convince you to agree with me as it is to moderate a conversation that enables you to arrive at conclusions about your own use of sermon illustrations. [10]

---

10. By including a quote from an author, I am not endorsing their theology or point of view. Neither do I expect all of my readers will share my theological point of view.

The book also presents findings from the second phase, which was to define eight types of sermon illustrations and determine the relative frequency with which preachers were using them. While this research is not definitive, it does provide a helpful framework for a balanced approach.

Before conducting the research, I'd noticed that preachers tend to have a default illustration type that they use more frequently than others. My default is "fresh illustrations," which are drawn from current events or popular culture. In January of 2000, I launched Fresh Sermon Illustrations, an illustration subscription service hosted at FreshMinistry.org. The goal was to give preachers an alternative to the canned illustrations found in anthology books. In an ironic twist, these illustrations are now available in print form and in the WordSearch, Accordance, and Logos software programs in nine different books.[11] More than twenty years of editing or writing thirty fresh sermon illustrations a month demonstrates my commitment to this type of sermon illustration and exposes a bias.

However, I've noticed my students favoring personal illustrations. Certainly, they use other types of illustrations in their sermons, but not with the same frequency with which they use personal stories—sometimes raw, unflattering stories of their own sinfulness, failures, and doubts. Transparency and honest self-disclosure drive their choice in sermon illustrations.

This is not limited to an isolated student every now and then. It is a pattern. I began to wonder if it was because of a generational divide. Or maybe it was because I was so heavily invested in fresh illustrations that my preferences were the anomaly. In addition, I observed that some of my contemporaries prefer historical

---

11. For a listing of books, go to www.freshministry.org. The entire illustration collection is available at www.freshsermonillustrations.net and https://sermons.faithlife.com.

illustrations, while others almost exclusively use biblical illustrations. What about the broader community—what kind of sermon illustrations were other preachers using?

Instead of relying on intuition or observation to answer these questions, I led a research team to conduct a study of randomly selected sermons from the collection hosted at sermons.faithlife.com to determine how frequently preachers were using different types of illustrations.

The selection criteria were sermon manuscripts uploaded as Word documents to sermons.faithlife.com by preachers from evangelical churches. While the small sample size does not provide statistical certainty, and a study with different selection criteria would likely yield different results, it does reveal a pattern.[12] While there is no statistically significant difference between the 20-percent frequency of biblical illustrations and the 19-percent frequency of hypothetical illustrations, the difference between the frequently used cluster, which contains rates from 19 to 24 percent, and the infrequently used cluster, which ranges between 1 and 6 percent, is significant. That gap is so large that even with a small sample, it is a meaningful distinction.

---

12. This sample size was a hundred sermons.

Frequently Used Cluster

Type	Definition	Frequency
Personal illustration	A story based on the preacher's own experiences	24%
Fresh illustration	From current events, recent publications, or popular movies	22%
Biblical illustration	Summarizes a story or event from the Bible	20%
Hypothetical illustration	Poses what-if questions or provides hypothetical examples	19%

Infrequently Used Cluster

Type	Definition	Frequency
Historical illustration	Summarizes an event or character from history or literature	6%
Classic illustration	A commonly used older story	6%
Fictional illustration	A made-up story (aka preacher's story)	3%
Object lesson	Includes the use of a physical object, diagram, or image that is in the preacher's hand or pointed to by the preacher while illustrating the point	1%

In some ways, the study confirmed what I had already observed, but some of the findings surprised me. I was not surprised that the preachers in the sample group:

- Used some types of illustrations more than others.

- Frequently used personal illustrations, fresh illustrations, and biblical illustrations.

- Used an average of 2.43 sermon illustrations per sermon. This frequency aligned with my own practice and what I've observed among my students and coaching clients.

However, I was surprised that the preachers in the sample group:

- Seldom used classic illustrations and fictional illustrations. I should say that I was pleasantly surprised by this finding. In both cases, my view is that these types of illustrations should only be used as a last resort.

- Made effective, frequent use of hypothetical illustrations.

- Did not use historical illustrations as much as I thought they would (or should).

Because 85 percent of the illustrations used in the sermons studied fell into the frequently used cluster, most of the second section of the book is dedicated to illustration types that the preachers used the most. However, because the second cluster represents 15–16 percent of the illustrations used, and because of the margin of error represented by the small sample size, I will devote some space to the other illustration types.

The chapters in section 2 will examine each illustration type in the order in which they appear in the frequency chart above. I will include examples of my sermon illustrations and those others have used and will analyze their effectiveness based on the findings in the first section. The footnotes provide links so you can see each illustration in the full context of the sermon.

Now, we begin by asking, "What makes an illustration effective?"

Section 1

Using Sermon Illustrations Effectively

1

Four Metaphors for Sermon Illustrations

Preachers and homileticians often use metaphors (or similes)[1] to speak about how illustrations function in sermons: bridges, windows, light, and pictures. While each of these falls short of capturing the full essence of sermon illustrations' efficacy, they all contribute to our understanding of how illustrations function in a sermon.

Sermon Illustrations as Bridges

When used well, sermon illustrations build a bridge from the familiar to the unfamiliar, the clear to the unclear, the known to the unknown, and, ultimately, the people to the message. Paul's sermon at Mars Hill (Acts 17) is a good example.

At the time of his visit to Athens, Paul was not on trial for his beliefs or behavior (that would come later), but he was asked to defend his views on Jesus and the resurrection before the Court of the Areopagus—a gathering of intellectuals with jurisdiction over educational and religious thought. The pressure was on. In

---

1. Technically, some of the following are similes because they contain the words "like" or "as." However, I chose not to go back and forth between the two words (metaphor and simile).

this intimidating arena of high culture, he was surrounded by accomplished rhetoricians. He was not one of them. By reputation (2 Cor 10:10) and his own admission (2 Cor 11:6), Paul was not a skilled speaker. However, his sermon on Mars Hill is a masterpiece of persuasive preaching and a model for how to use illustrations to overcome communication obstacles. Paul's sermon illustration worked in concert with the rest of his sermon. From beginning to end, Paul worked to move the people from what they already knew to what he wanted to teach them:

> Paul stood in the middle of the Areopagus and said, "People of Athens! I see that you are extremely religious in every respect. For as I was passing through and observing the objects of your worship, I even found an altar on which was inscribed: 'To an Unknown God.' Therefore, what you worship in ignorance, this I proclaim to you. The God who made the world and everything in it—he is Lord of heaven and earth—does not live in shrines made by hands. Neither is he served by human hands, as though he needed anything, since he himself gives everyone life and breath and all things. From one man he has made every nationality to live over the whole earth and has determined their appointed times and the boundaries of where they live. He did this so that they might seek God, and perhaps they might reach out and find him, though he is not far from each one of us. For in him we live and move and have our being, as even some of your own poets have said, 'For we are also his offspring.' Since we are God's offspring then, we shouldn't think that the divine nature is like gold or silver or stone, an image fashioned by human art and imagination.

"Therefore, having overlooked the times of ignorance, God now commands all people everywhere to repent, because he has set a day when he is going to judge the world in righteousness by the man he has appointed. He has provided proof of this to everyone by raising him from the dead."

When they heard about the resurrection of the dead, some began to ridicule him, but others said, "We'd like to hear from you again about this." So Paul left their presence. However, some people joined him and believed, including Dionysius the Areopagite, a woman named Damaris, and others with them. (Acts 17:22–34)

Sermon illustrations do not stand alone. They interact with other sermon elements to accomplish the preacher's goal. In this case, Paul was introducing himself and his message in a cross-cultural ministry setting. He was on his audience's turf, not his, and he needed to connect personally with them and then preach the gospel before he could call on them to act on its claims. Notice how Paul's illustration functions in the sermon, working with the other elements to connect the people to the speaker, the message, and, ultimately, to God.

In the introduction, Paul connects with his audience by setting the proper tone and preparing them to hear his message. Though the multiple idols he encountered in the city had troubled him (Acts 17:16), he frames his observation in an inoffensive way. He speaks of the citizens as being "extremely religious." In addition, Paul refers to the inscription on one of their idols "to an unknown god" to grab and hold their attention—he was in the Acropolis that day to tell them about the God they did not yet know. This is not to say that he put his stamp of approval on what he observed. He did not.[2] What he did was find a way for him to connect with them and them with him. Without the connection, the people would have immediately dismissed him, but worse still, they would have dismissed the gospel.

In the body of the sermon, he shares his deep theological convictions that their "unknown god" created the world (17:24a), is sovereign over all (24b), providentially cares for all (25), is responsible for all human life (26), is transcendent and yet personal (27), and is the center of creation's very existence (28a).

After stating his succinct, theologically rich message, he illustrates it with a reference to familiar literature: Greek poetry.[3] The illustration was familiar, clear, interesting, and appropriate for his audience, and as a result, it was convincing. Because he illustrated the message out of their world, he continued to bridge a relational gap between him and them, but he also created a bridge between their experiences and his message. Essentially, he helped them to understand an unfamiliar message by rooting it in what was known, loved, and already embraced in their culture—a bridge

---

2. "It is to be acknowledged, however, that whilst Paul does not stigmatize the culture, he does stop short of 'baptising' it. Graeco-Roman philosophy, poetry, and religiosity very clearly lie outside the parameters of the Christian kerygma and elements of each are only ever appropriated and used by Paul in the service of the Gospel. The matter of importance here is that of first principles. The missiologist and preacher par excellence of the first generation of Christianity, St Paul, is not reticent to enlist what we might call 'high culture' in service of his message; however there is nothing to suggest he ever took the view that the forces of culture and society should ever impose themselves upon the message." Billings, "As Some of Your Own Prophets Have Said," 484.

3. "First, Paul gave a quotation attributed to the Cretan poet Epimenides (*ca.* 600 BC) in his *Cretica*: 'For in thee we live and move and have our being.' Then he cited Cleanthes (331–233 BC), *Hymn to Zeus, 4*, and the Cilician poet Aratus (*ca.* 315–240 BC) in his *Phaenomena, 5*, 'for we are also his offspring.' " Mare, *New Testament Background Commentary,* 197–98.

from the familiar to the unfamiliar. The illustration helped them understand and relate to his message, which allowed them to apply it to their lives.

Paul pivots from the illustration to proclaim that God is not in idol form (29) and asks the listeners to turn away from idol worship and turn to him (30). He concludes by showing the relationship of what he has preached to the question at hand—the resurrection from the dead. The resurrection of Jesus Christ is the proof that God will be the final judge of all life (31).

Paul's sermon—encompassing the introduction, body (explanation and illustration), and the conclusion—was effective. The full force of the message resulted in some hearers embracing the message and becoming Christ followers (34). Specifically, the illustration he used made the explanation more accessible and believable to them. It was consistent with his tone and tied the whole sermon together. Throughout the sermon, Paul tore down obstacles and built bridges. He did it especially well with his sermon illustration. Good illustrations—well-chosen, appropriate illustrations—do that; they bridge understanding, culture, and worldviews to help listeners understand, apply, and experience the message.

Sermon Illustrations as Windows

People often use the metaphor of windows in everyday conversation. In modern parlance, we speak of:

- windows of opportunity—a short time to accomplish something

- windows on the world—going past a provincial point of view

- window dressing—a frivolous decoration that adds no depth

- window shopping—just looking without being intent on buying

- flying out the window—a missed opportunity.

While each of these might add to our understanding of sermon illustrations (for instance, illustrations can prop up a poor sermon and essentially become window dressing), Charles Spurgeon used the window metaphor to emphasize two aspects of sermon illustrations: 1) they let in light and 2) they allow fresh air to circulate. In *Lectures to My Students*, he writes:

> A building without windows would be a prison rather than a house, for it would be quite dark, and no one would care to take it upon lease; and, in the same way, a discourse without a parable is prosy and dull, and involves a grievous weariness of the flesh. ... Our congregations hear us with pleasure when we give them a fair measure of imagery: when an anecdote is being told, they rest, take breath, and give play to their imaginations, and thus prepare themselves for the sterner work, which lies before them in listening to our profounder expositions.[4]

Spurgeon's window metaphor explains that sermon illustrations bring light into the room, keeping the sermon from feeling like a prison. The etymology of the word "illustration" involves the casting of light,[5] so it is appropriate that Spurgeon uses a meta-

---

4. Spurgeon, *Lectures to My Students*, 2.

5. "The word 'illustration,' comes from the Latin *illustrare*, meaning 'to cast light upon.' In short, illustrations clarify meaning and as such are key

phor that includes shining light on the biblical truth.[6] That is also how twentieth-century homiletics professor Andrew Blackwood utilizes the metaphor: "A first-class illustration is like a window which lets the morning sunlight stream into the dining room. A poor illustration is like a sham window which admits no light, and permits no person to look out."[7] Blackwood uses the metaphor to differentiate between first-class and poor illustrations. The effective ones let in the light; ineffective ones block a person's view.

The observation that windows let in light does not exhaust the usefulness of the window metaphor. Windows do not simply let light in; they also allow a refreshing breeze to circulate in a room. Spurgeon's quote spends very little space speaking of light but a great deal speaking of the breeze. Without the illustrations, the sermon's prose would be "dull," and it would make the flesh of the listeners "weary." Just as a cool breeze coming through a window is refreshing on a sweltering day, sermon illustrations refresh the mind so it can grasp weightier matters. Spurgeon goes so far as to say that without the window, people would likely stay home and read instead of listening to a sermon "made up of solid slabs of doctrine."[8]

Spurgeon uses the window metaphor from the perspective of being in the room seeing the light and feeling the breeze. Others have expanded the metaphor by shifting the point of view to

---

components in explaining the text. Constructing a sermon without illustrations is like building a house without windows. It is no wonder congregations often fail to see the point of sermons when illustrations are absent." Charette, "Keeping Your People Glued," 44.

6. "Often when didactic speech fails to enlighten our hearers we may make them see our meaning by opening a window and letting in the pleasant light of analogy." Spurgeon, *Lectures to My Students,* 13.

7. Blackwood, *Preaching from the Bible,* 189.

8. Spurgeon, *Lectures to My Students,* 3.

the outside looking in. "Illustrations are like the windows of a house. They allow you to look inside, see, and remember what you saw."[9] Sermon illustrations do more than provide light; they provide insight.

Sermon Illustrations as Lights

The window metaphor includes light, inasmuch as a window lets light into a room. However, many preachers and homileticians use light as a standalone metaphor for sermon illustrations. To some, shedding light makes "the meaning plain";[10] to others, it "clarifies"[11] or "illumines" the truth.[12] Veteran pastor Silas Krueger uses the light metaphor to speak of the effect of an illustration to enlighten "once-darkened minds."[13] So ultimately, the light metaphor shows that sermon illustrations function to highlight the text and enlighten the minds of the hearers.

---

9. Akin, Curtis, and Rummage, *Engaging Exposition*, loc. 3316.

10. "The word illustrate means 'to cast light upon something.' When used regarding preaching, it refers to those elements in a sermon which by analogy, in a general sense, allow the hearer to grasp more precisely the meaning the preacher intends." Hamilton, *Homiletical Handbook*, 51. "By illustrating the sermon, we are able to shed light on the text and make its meaning plain, establish an emotional connection with our hearers, and provide a hook by which they can remember and apply the exhortations of the sermon." York and Decker, *Preaching with Bold Assurance,* 150.

11. "The way to cast light on the truth is through an illustration. In fact, the word illustration actually means to enlighten or make clear." Merida, *Faithful Preaching,* 107. "In the proper sense of the term, an illustration refers to that which illumines or clarifies what has been said another way." Craddock, *Preaching,* 203.

12. "Remember that the goal of an illustration is to illuminate God's truth." Carter, Duvall, and Hays, *Preaching God's Word,* 135. "An illustration never establishes a truth—it illuminates a truth." Larsen, *Anatomy of Preaching,* 79.

13. Krueger, "Preaching in an Oral Age," 99.

The light metaphor not only provides guidance for what illustrations do; it also warns of a potential threat that arises from using inappropriate illustrations: to overpower the sermon's message. Seminary professor Murray Capill writes:

> By definition an illustration is intended to throw light on a subject. If the light itself draws all the attention, it is self-defeating. When people leave after a message, remembering some great stories and anecdotes, but unable to recall what the stories illustrated, they have effectively looked into a floodlight while failing to see the building that was being lit up.[14]

The window metaphor offers the same warning. While it is common to open a window to allow a fresh breeze into a house on a warm day, no one would open it during a hurricane. However, the light metaphor more powerfully highlights the possibility of an illustration being a distraction. Illustrations are capable of having the exact opposite of their intended effect: instead of helping listeners understand, apply, or experience the message, they can draw attention away from the point of the text or block a listener from hearing what is being said. Preaching professor Haddon Robinson says:

> The word illustration means "to throw light on a subject." Effective illustrations are like footlights that help us see the actors on the stage. But if a footlight shines in the audience's eyes, it blinds them to what they ought to see. A story told for its own sake may entertain or amuse, but if it fails to throw light on the truth preached, it is not an

---

14. Capill, *Preaching with Spiritual Vigour*, 179.

"illustration" but simply a story. It gets in the way. In fact, the better the story, the more distracting it will likely be.[15]

I experienced this phenomenon in a painful way a few years ago. In the first few months of serving as a transitional pastor in a Southern California church, I used the following illustration to introduce a Christmas sermon on Mary, the mother of Jesus. In it, I told the story of visiting a historic Catholic church in Santa Fe while on a tour:

> As we entered, I noticed a class in an adjacent room and was happy to see praying people sprinkled throughout the building. Yes, the confessional booths and statues made me feel a little uneasy, but I overcame the uneasiness to enjoy the distinct architecture and superior craftsmanship of the historic building—it was impressive.
>
> I was really enjoying the tour until we meandered into a room that contained a shrine to Mary. Beneath the artist's rendition of our Lord's mother knelt a woman who was obviously praying to Mary. I couldn't get out of there fast enough.
>
> I've known for years that some Catholics pray to Mary, but knowing it and seeing it are two different things. How sad that people misunderstand the Christmas story and worship Mary instead of her Son.[16]

---

15. Robinson, "What Sermon Illustrations Should Be Banned from Pulpits?," 31.

16. Jim L. Wilson, "Mary's Treasure: Her Son Was Also Her Savior," https://sermons.faithlife.com/sermons/80078-mary's-treasure:-her-son-was-also-her-savior. In the examples I will be using, I will be correcting obvious grammatical and spelling errors without using sic. Also, the resources from sermons.faithlife.com and blogs will not be listed in the bibliography but will have fuller citation information in their footnotes.

When I preached the sermon, I was more descriptive and emotive, including saying that seeing this woman pray to Mary made me feel sick to my stomach. As it turns out, I miscalculated the appropriateness of this illustration for this congregation.

Within a few weeks, a staff member's husband made an appointment to see me. Because I had been in the church such a short time, there was much about him I did not know, including that he and many of those who attended the church were former Catholics.

He began the meeting with, "We're leaving the church." My jaw dropped. "A couple of weeks ago when you were describing walking through that historic church in Santa Fe, it was as if I was walking alongside you, seeing what you saw, hearing the sounds you heard, and smelling what you were smelling." He continued, "When you described the little lady praying at the altar, I immediately saw my mother, faithfully practicing her faith." He went on to say that he was shocked to hear my response—that *she* made me sick to my stomach. (This was not what I said, but it is what he heard.)

He personalized the story. He experienced the story. He put a face—his mother's—on the woman I saw. I made a poor homiletical choice. I used an illustration that did not shine a light on the text. Instead, it blinded him (and others) to the sermon. It was not appropriate in this context.

We were able to work through his frustration, and his family did not leave the church. In fact, we were able to rebuild trust to the point that several months later he brought his mother with him to a worship service and introduced her to me. That is the good news—a gracious man was able to forgive his pastor for making a poor choice in sermon illustrations. But the bad news is that he couldn't hear a word I spoke after the illustration that blinded him to the truth that emerged from the text.

Do not get me wrong; I still believe that people should not pray to Mary. But in this case, the introduction failed to shine the light on the text; instead, it prevented this man, and perhaps others, from hearing the message of the sermon.

Sermon Illustrations as Pictures

In recent years, another metaphor has emerged to explain a sermon illustration's function: a picture. The media age has moved people toward thinking in pictures, not just words.[17] Daniel Akin, Bill Curtis, and Stephen Rummage write, "The use of illustration recognizes that people more readily grab hold of pictures and images than they do propositions. However, the purpose of a picture or an image is to shed light on the proposition or principle that undergirds the picture."[18] In the same way that the light metaphor includes making the truth clearer, so does the picture metaphor. Robinson writes, "An illustration, like the picture on television, makes clear what the speaker explains."[19]

Even before the rise of the electronic media, this metaphor worked. People commonly refer to pictures, graphs, charts, or any visual depictions of a concept in a book as illustrations. Illustrations help to make the abstract concrete and give a representation of how a concept plays out in reality.

---

17. "Illustrations are needed in sermons. They are needed to reach the present-day visually oriented mind. Our generation has been trained to think in pictures. Children are taught to read by using visual aids. The earliest lessons in school are learned through the devices of visual projection. Movies, television, and computers have trained the modern mind to think in pictures and to receive information from electronic screens. Minds so trained will not listen through a sermon wholly dependent on logical thought to covey [*sic*] its meaning. People need word pictures in preaching, too." Brown et al., *Steps to the Sermon,* 82–84.

18. Akin, Curtis, and Rummage, *Engaging Exposition*, loc. 3361.

19. Robinson, *Biblical Preaching*, 152.

Picture, in this case, is a metaphor—not an actual image projected on a screen. It occurs in the mind. The words used evoke a picture that illustrates a concept in the mind just as an artist would illustrate a concept in a book with a drawing.

However, with the rise of the electronic media, pictures are no longer just a metaphor for illustrations but can become the form of the illustration. We will explore the specifics of using media clips in the chapter on fresh illustrations (chapter 5).

Illustrations have a rich tradition in the biblical narrative and the history of preaching. Bridges, windows, lights, and pictures are metaphors that explain how they contribute to effective communication in the sermon. They also caution that illustrations can become obstacles to effective meaning transmission. Not all illustrations are helpful, which prompts the question, "How can I ensure that illustrations add to the message instead of taking away from it?" Or, to put it another way, "What makes sermon illustrations effective?"

2

Four Characteristics of Effective Sermon Illustrations

They say that beauty is in the eye of the beholder. What one finds beautiful, another does not. The same is true about sermon illustrations. To some degree, evaluating the potential effectiveness of a sermon illustration is subjective, a matter of personal preference.

For years, I have given students an assignment of reading through a collection of illustrations and bringing a favorite to share with the class. What one student finds helpful, another does not. If I were given this assignment, I think I would bring this illustration:

> Simon Wiesenthal, an Austrian Jew, spent four and a half years in various Nazi concentration camps during World War II. Wiesenthal, one of the few to survive the atrocities of the Holocaust, recounts a harrowing story in his memoir *The Sunflower*. While working to clear rubbish from a makeshift hospital, a nurse summoned Wiesenthal to a secret room, where a severely wounded Nazi soldier lay on his deathbed. The soldier told Wiesenthal how he volunteered for the SS (Schutzstaffel) and how his superiors ordered him to gun down innocent Jews. Wiesenthal listened to the soldier as he expressed deep sorrow and

regret for what he had done. He said that he wanted to confess his sin to a Jew before he died. Wiesenthal, unable to offer any comforting words of forgiveness, left the room in silence.

Unfortunately, the soldier confessed his sin to the wrong Jew. There is a Jew who would not walk out of the room unable to offer forgiveness. Jesus Christ is willing and able to forgive the sins of all who come to him with a sincere heart and a desire to change (Mark 2:5–12).[1]

I like many things about this illustration. I like the contrast between, on the one hand, the hopelessness of the soldier needing forgiveness and the helplessness of the hospital worker who could not offer it and, on the other hand, the power of Jesus Christ, who made forgiveness possible. Just as a sparkling diamond looks even more brilliant against a black backdrop, the despair in this illustration highlights Jesus's ability to offer hope. All these observations are subjective, though. I like the illustration; you may not.

While one's opinion of sermon illustrations is subjective in some ways, there are more objective criteria for evaluating their effectiveness. In my team's research, we found four characteristics of effective sermon illustrations. They are *familiar*, *clear*, *interesting*, and *appropriate*.

---

1. Jim L. Wilson and Loren C. Pirtle, "Simon Wiesenthal Unable to Extend Forgiveness to Dying German Soldier," https://sermons.faithlife.com /sermons/121977-simon-wiesenthal-unable-to-extend-forgiveness-to-dying -german-soldier.

Using the Sermon Illustration
Evaluation Rubric

The table on the following page uses a green light (go), yellow light (caution), and red light (stop) framework for each characteristic to help preachers predict a specific illustration's potential effectiveness.

If a sermon illustration has a single red light, I would not recommend using it. Find another way to illustrate the text. However, that does not mean all four characteristics need to be green-lighted. If a yellow light appears, attempt to mitigate the possible obstacle by rewriting the illustration (without changing the facts).

Later in the chapter, you will find an explanation of each characteristic, but for now, take a moment to read the rubric, and then use it to evaluate the Wiesenthal illustration.

Here's my evaluation using the rubric:

Familiar: Green light. The Holocaust, though it happened years ago, is familiar to most audiences. Though most people were not alive when it occurred, members would have encountered references to it in history books and in pop culture. Even if congregation members were not familiar with the historic events, most would relate to the struggle to forgive someone who has wronged them or to the desire for forgiveness.

Clear: Green light. The setup to the story and the inner struggle Wiesenthal experienced are easy to follow/experience/understand. The illustration is clear, crisp, and concise. The illustration has a reliable source and is likely an accurate representation of what happened.

Interesting: Green light. The angst of the soldier, his urgency to ask for forgiveness on his deathbed, and Wiesenthal's abrupt response of walking out of the room without speaking introduce a palpable tension, which releases with the unexpected reversal: "Unfortunately, the soldier confessed his sin to the wrong Jew."

	Red light	Yellow light	Green light
Familiar	It is **not likely** that **any** members in the congregation will be familiar with, know about, identify with, or have a connection with the illustration.	It is **possible** that **many** members in the congregation will be familiar with, know about, identify with, or have a connection with the illustration.	It is **probable** that **most** members in the congregation will be familiar with, know about, identify with, or have a connection with the illustration.
Clear	The illustration is **not clear**, has **inaccurate details**, or does not **parallel the text**.	The illustration contains **details** that may make it hard to follow.	The illustration is **void of needless and inaccurate details** and has an **evident connection** to the text.
Interesting	It is **probable** that the illustration will upstage the text.	It is **possible** that the illustration will upstage the text.	The illustration is **likely** to stimulate interest in the text.
Appropriate	It is **probable** that someone in the primary or secondary audience will be offended or that the story breaks confidences.	It is **possible** that someone in the primary or secondary audience will be offended.	The illustration is **not likely** to offend members of the primary or secondary audience. The story does not break confidences.

Appropriate: Yellow light. Because the illustration does not elaborate on horrific details of the Holocaust, and the severe wounds the soldier suffered are not described, the illustration would be appropriate in most situations. However, references to the Holocaust can be risky and could be offensive to some members of a secondary audience (for more on secondary audiences, see below). In addition, even though the SS member said that he wanted to confess to a "Jew," the illustration can come off to the modern listener as insensitive. If I were to use this illustration in a sermon, I would change the final paragraph to say, "Unfortunately, the soldier confessed his sin to the wrong ~~Jew~~ **person**. There is ~~a Jew~~ **someone** who would not walk out of the room unable to offer forgiveness. Jesus Christ is willing and able to forgive the sins of all who come to him with a sincere heart and a desire to change (Mark 2:5–12)."

Overall, the illustration functions to introduce the audience to Jesus's capacity to forgive sins, which is questioned by the scribes in Mark 2:5–12. Beyond that, it affirms that Jesus can forgive even horrific sins of great sinners.

However, your evaluation could be different based on the congregation where you would use the illustration. Notice that the rubric calls for an evaluation of how a specific congregation will likely hear it. An illustration could work in one setting and not in another.

Effective Illustrations Are Familiar

The bridge metaphor works well to describe this characteristic. If an illustration is to function as a bridge from the known to the unknown—from something that people already understand to something they are learning—then it must be familiar and understood to the audience;[2] otherwise, it becomes a barrier to understanding the text.

To be effective, the illustration (its content, context, and subject) must be in the congregation's consciousness—it must be familiar. If the listeners are not already familiar with an illustration, it will not help them understand, apply, or experience the text.

Familiar to the congregation, not just the preacher. Senior Preaching Lecturer Adrian Lane writes, "A classic mistake for preachers is to draw all their illustrations from their own world, whether it be the sporting, active, outdoor world of some, the domestic, relational world of others, or the ethical, political world of yet others. As a preacher, one needs to be attuned to the worlds of one's listeners, discerning their experience and how they communicate."[3]

This is especially important for preachers engaged in a non-homogeneous ministry or who have eclectic interests. For example, a preacher who is a sci-fi fan may often see a connection between his favorite sci-fi trilogy and the text, but if his congregation does not share this interest, they will check out during the weekly sci-fi illustration. This is particularly true with things like sci-fi (few people are neutral on sci-fi; either they love it or they hate it) or politics (few people are neutral in their political views).

Beyond niche interests, a preacher's gender creates some bias. When I was a senior pastor preaching to the same congregation each week, I would purchase books written by popular women authors and ask female church members to read them

---

2. "The aim of an illustration is to explain the unknown with the known, the distant with the familiar." Robinson, *Biblical Preaching*, 157. "Illustrations use something people do understand to explain what they don't understand." Moyer, *Show Me How to Illustrate Evangelistic Sermons*, 14.

3. Lane, "The God Who Illustrates," 341.

and underline what they found meaningful. I would then look through the highlights and use them as the basis for sermon illustrations. I did this because I was aware that my illustrations were not always relatable to women in the congregation.

This principle is not just about gender. Younger pastors could do the same with older church members, as could older pastors with young adults. Today there is a trend toward pastors of larger churches having "teaching teams," meaning that they submit their sermon manuscript prior to preaching it to a team of others who critique and offer suggestions for illustrations that relate to specific demographics in the congregation in an effort to ensure that the sermon illustrations are familiar.

The power of familiarity. In the 2018–19 academic year, I taught preaching at three different locations: online, on Gateway Seminary's main campus in Ontario, California, and on the Rocky Mountain campus in Denver, Colorado. The online class had students from around the world. The two face-to-face classes each had a distinct flavor, both being primarily populated by students who lived in their respective regions. I gave each class the assignment that introduced this chapter: read a collection of sermon illustrations, bring a favorite back to class, and share why they liked it. The students from the online and California classes had a wider variety of selections than the Rocky Mountain group did. About half of the Colorado students selected the same illustration:

> On November 12, 2006, Frank, a follower of Christ, and his wife Becca were walking in Denver with their two children, Macie, four years old, and Garrison, two. Mom and dad were pushing Macie and Garrison in a side-by-side stroller. As they crossed an intersection, a drunk driver, Lawrence Trujillo, ran the red light and hit the family. The impact killed Becca and the two kids instantly. It seriously

wounded Frank. Trujillo never looked back. Instead, he thought it the best thing to repair his damaged grille and hide the truck.

The Denver community ached at the horrid news. It watched Frank intently to see how he would react to the loss of his family and to Trujillo. A week later, Frank left the hospital and attended the funeral of his wife and two children. Twelve hundred people crammed into Colorado Community Church. One of Frank's friends wrote about the service:

> Frank's minister spoke for Frank at the funeral. Frank wanted to encourage us to move beyond our anger and try to find a way to forgive Mr. Trujillo. He asked us to recognize that the Trujillo family was also destroyed that night. ... Frank set his intention to take the moral high road and asked that we join him in finding a way to forgive. The depth of Frank's character stopped me cold.

In his darkest hour, Frank strove to point the Denver community to God by living in obedience to Christ's instruction to forgive those who have wronged us.

In November 2007, several news agencies were thrilled to gain interviews with Frank and ask him how he was doing with his trials a year later. Frank said, "I know that harboring unforgiveness can eat away at a person, and I don't want that. ... I am trying to hang on to the positives, however few I can find. I don't always feel that way. I am making a conscious effort each day." According to one interviewer, Frank "is just trying to take one step at a time and is leaning on his faith. He remembers something he read recently: 'Faith that hasn't been tested can't be trusted.' This test will last a lifetime." In another interview, Frank revealed that he regularly struggles between asking "Why me?" and "Why my family?" and letting God use this trial in his life to bring glory to His name.

Clearly, Frank Bingham demonstrates that coming to a God-centered perspective in life's trials is painful and difficult. It is a process founded on the grace and strength of the Lord in our lives. Many aspects of Christian growth will have accompanying growing pains. We have committed to each other to pursue depth in Christ together. Are we still willing to move from the status quo even if it is painful? This is the question for us to consider this morning. Too many Christians are resistant in their Christian development because they are comfortable. Yet Christ offers us a surpassing richness if we will move to him (Matt 6:14–15).[4]

I do not recall any students from the online or California classes selecting this illustration as their favorite one in the collection, but several in the Colorado class did. Why? Certainly it is a compelling story that illustrates that it is possible to live out Matthew 6:14–15 and forgive wrongdoers, but it is also very long—at five hundred words, it would occupy about a quarter of a thirty-minute sermon, and for that reason alone it might be rejected by most preachers when selecting a way to illustrate Matthew 6:14–15. In addition, the illustration was no longer fresh—after twelve years, even the freshest of illustrations has grown a little stale.

---

4. Jim L. Wilson and Doug Jones, "Man Forgives Drunk Driver for Killing His Family," https://sermons.faithlife.com/sermons/108651 -man-forgives-drunk-driver-for-killing-his-family.

When I asked the Colorado students why they liked this illustration so much, they responded, "Because we remember this story, and so would most of the people in our congregations. We lived through these events, and they strike a chord with us."

Beyond it being familiar, it was relatable to them—it involved more than their heads; it stimulated their hearts.[5] Pastor Timothy Keller writes, "The essence of a good illustration, then, is to evoke a remembered sense experience and bring it into connection with a principle. That makes the truth real both by helping listeners better understand it and by inclining their hearts more to love it."[6] This happened in a very concrete way for the Colorado students. The illustration did not merely parallel an experience they shared, it referred to an experience they lived through, which helped them experience the text more fully.[7]

The example of Jesus. Jesus's illustrations were almost always from common, everyday elements from the world of his listeners.[8] A good example is the hypothetical illustration he used to close out the Sermon on the Mount:

---

5. "A well-chosen illustration will usually get the hearer to nod his head and say, 'I understand what you're saying.' A story that engages the hearer on the emotional as well as the intellectual level will move that same hearer to say, 'I agree with what you are saying.' He will feel the lesson of your story, not just grasp it." Krueger, "Preaching in an Oral Age," 99.

6. Keller, *Preaching: Communicating Faith in an Age of Skepticism*, 173.

7. "Illustrations are therefore doors that preachers open to allow listeners to experience a concept; and by experiencing it, to understand it, interact with it, and act upon it." Chapell, *Using Illustrations to Preach with Power*, 39. "This use of experienced truth will also assist engagement and therefore learning in general. Chiefly this is due to identification and pertinence. It will also be due to inherent interest and variety in communication mode." Lane, "The God Who Illustrates," 335.

8. "He [Jesus] used down-to-earth images and illustrations that appealed to the common people because they were drawn from everyday life: the farm,

Therefore, everyone who hears these words of mine and acts on them will be like a wise man who built his house on the rock. The rain fell, the rivers rose, and the winds blew and pounded that house. Yet it didn't collapse, because its foundation was on the rock. But everyone who hears these words of mine and doesn't act on them will be like a foolish man who built his house on the sand. The rain fell, the rivers rose, the winds blew and pounded that house, and it collapsed. It collapsed with a great crash. (Matt 7:24–27)

Jesus used what was commonly understood—a strong foundation that is hard to build but will withstand storms—to help his audience grasp a parallel thought. Listening but not applying the teaching is easy, like building on sand, but it will not be beneficial. On the other hand, listening and applying the teaching is difficult, like working with a stone foundation, but it will endure even the direst of situations.

Sermon illustrations must be familiar before they can help the people understand, apply,[9] or experience[10] the text. In eval-

---

the economy, the home, the marketplace." Capill, *Preaching with Spiritual Vigour,* 168. "He [Christ] drew illustrations entirely from things familiar with his hearers." Broadus, *Lectures on the History of Preaching,* 24–25.

9. "By use of a story, quote, metaphor, historical reference, or the like, the preacher gives some concrete flesh to the abstract proposition. Without the use of such illustrations, the sermon could almost be a theological or ethical lecture. But the illustrations help hearers assimilate the abstract theology or ethics and connect them to real life, that is, 'apply' them to their very real lives." Allen, *Determining the Form,* 23.

10. "Illustrations are 'life-situation' stories within sermons whose details (whether explicitly told or imaginatively elicited) allow listeners to identify with an experience that elaborates, develops, and explains scriptural principles." Chapell, *Using Illustrations to Preach with Power,* 21. See also Krueger, "Preaching in an Oral Age," 109: "A good story not only grabs the attention of the hearers;

uating how familiar your congregation will be with the people, events, or subject matter of the illustration, you can use the following guide:

Red light	Yellow light	Green light
It is **not likely** that **any** members in the congregation will be familiar with, know about, identify with, or have a connection with the illustration.	It is **possible** that **many** members in the congregation will be familiar with, know about, identify with, or have a connection with the illustration.	It is **probable** that **most** members in the congregation will be familiar with, know about, identify with, or have a connection with the illustration.

Effective Illustrations Are Clear

In the same way that illustrations about known and familiar things can help explain unfamiliar concepts in the text, illustrations can also work to make the biblical truth clearer to the audience.[11] Clarity builds on familiarity. If it is familiar, there is a greater chance that it will be clear to the listeners—but it is not a guarantee.

The picture metaphor helps explain this characteristic. The illustration serves as an example or picture of the sermon point, biblical truth, or principle. It presents a concrete expression of an abstract thought—a demonstration that helps the congregation

---

it also touches their emotions. Through the use of stories you can help the congregation experience what your sermon teaches."

11. "The purpose of an illustration is to make the truth clearer to the listener." Wiersbe and Wiersbe, *The Elements of Preaching*, 86.

visualize how the principle works in real life. Good illustrations parallel the text closely, making the abstract more concrete, as Anglican minister John Stott says:

> Such is the purpose of every illustration, of whatever kind. It is to stimulate people's imagination and to help them to see things clearly in their minds. Illustrations transform the abstract into the concrete, the ancient into the modern, the unfamiliar into the familiar, the general into the particular, the vague into the precise, the unreal into the real, and the invisible into the visible.[12]

They clarify the topic, yes, but they also make the application of the text crystal clear to the audience. According to pastor and author Sidney Greidanus, "Whatever the source, one ought to select illustrations not simply to create interest but to elucidate the truth or to concretize the application of a particular passage."[13]

But for the illustration to help the text, it must be clear itself. Some people are good storytellers. Others are not; they have to work at it. I'm thinking especially of those who provide too many extraneous details. Lane points this out:

> Too many stories in sermons are cluttered with extraneous details. This is sometimes to foster interest and engagement. However, it makes it difficult for the audience to locate the truth. Details need to be rigorously pruned so that only the details pertinent to the truth's

---

12. Stott, *Between Two Worlds,* 239.

13. Greidanus, *The Modern Preacher and the Ancient Text,* 340–41. "Illustrations bring clarity to biblical truth and reveal how God's Word works and has worked in the lives of others." Akin, Curtis, and Rummage, *Engaging Exposition,* loc 3339.

communication are included, in appropriate proportion. Listeners can thereby plainly discern the truth conveyed. [14]

Limiting the number of details will improve the clarity of an illustration. If you include extraneous details, you not only lengthen the illustration, taking valuable time away from biblical exposition, but you also run the risk of shifting focus away from the point the story is illustrating to the illustration itself.

In the manuscript preparation stage, preachers should go through their illustrations (and their exposition for that matter) and delete any extraneous words. Instead of embellishing or stretching, they should make the illustration as concise as possible. Avoid needless words so people can follow the sermon better and see the biblical truth more clearly. Clear the fog.

Another important caution about details: make sure you get them right. If a fact sounds off to a listener, they might fact-check you on the spot. Details must be accurate. If they are inaccurate, you will lose credibility with those who notice.

Details matter, whether the subject of the illustration is from pop culture,[15] history,[16] or nature.[17] The loss of credibility in even

---

14. Lane, "The God Who Illustrates," 336.

15. "However, if I as a preacher mangle the facts about the pop-culture world, I lose points. It's okay if I admit I don't know. But if I act like I know and I don't, then I lose points." Miller, "3 Questions to Ask When Preaching from Pop Culture."

16. "When we seek illustrative or supportive material in the fields of astronomy or American history, for example, we often find one source, grab what we need, and go with it. In the end, the history major or the high school astronomy teacher hears our erroneous depiction of his or her field and assumes we don't do our homework. Now our entire week of work is held in suspicion—all because of our lackadaisical preparation in ancillary areas." Fabarez, *Preaching That Changes Lives*, 136.

17. "I once used an illustration about snakes and referred to them as 'slimy, poisonous creatures.' A woman came up afterward and said, 'Snakes aren't

the unimportant elements will cause you to lose credibility in general. Preaching professor Donald Hamilton says, "It is imperative that illustrations be presented with accuracy. If this is not done, credibility is damaged."[18] If you are not sure about a detail, let the people know, but don't fake it.

If the illustrations are not clear because of extraneous or erroneous details, it will be impossible for them to clarify the text. In evaluating the clarity of an illustration, you can use the following guide:

Red light	Yellow light	Green light
The illustration is **not clear**, has **inaccurate details**, or does not **parallel the text**.	The illustration contains **details** that may make it hard to follow.	The illustration is **void of needless and inaccurate details** and has an **evident connection** to the text.

Effective Illustrations Are Interesting

One of the ways the window metaphor serves our understanding of sermon illustrations' function is by highlighting the need for illustrations to create interest in the exegesis. While some have expressed displeasure with Spurgeon's window metaphor and his insistence on using illustrations,[19] he nonetheless emphasized the

---

slimy; they are dry. And most snakes aren't poisonous.' She worked in a zoo, so she spotted that I was careless in my description. As a result, I had given her reason for suspecting the rest of what I had to say." Robinson, *Making a Difference in Preaching*, 36.

18. Hamilton, *Preaching with Balance*, 275–76.

19. "We gospel proclaimers are told that the illustration is the 'window' to the sermon. It illuminates and supports our points, which are apparently

need for illustrations because they assist listeners in keeping their attention on the text.

Presbyterian minister and professor Bryan Chapell puts it this way:

> If the exposition goes on and on without rather immediate relevance at least beckoning, mental channels have changed to another station. If a Puritan model is appropriate for the subject, it is still necessary that the doctrinal development portions be chock-full of illustrations, allusions, and statements of applicational intent that will keep everyone tuned in. It will do little for the kingdom to blame the people for not responding if the preacher does less to help them listen.[20]

Illustrations tend to create interest in the text, in large part because of their narrative form. There is something inherently interesting about stories. Preaching professor O. C. Edwards writes, "More argument is advanced through narrative analogy than through closely reasoned expositions of concepts. Nothing perks up attention so much as a good story, and nothing is quite so persuasive as hearing the principle applied in an account of the lives of people."[21]

Maybe this is because stories represent our earliest form of communication;[22] maybe it is just a sign of the times, the way

---

so weak that they need help standing." Farmer, "What Sermon Illustrations Should Be Banned?," 31.

20.   Chapell, "Alternative Models," 124. See also Deuel, "Expository Preaching from Old Testament Narrative," 293–94: "Illustrations also keep the listeners' attention."

21.   Edwards, *Elements of Homiletic*, 90.

22.   "What is it about an illustration, or story, that holds people's attention and remains in their memory? Well, there seem to be several factors. As

twenty-first-century people prefer to get their information;[23] or, more in line with Spurgeon's window metaphor, maybe it's simply that stories provide a break for the listeners as they soak in the exegesis.[24] Regardless, sermon illustrations help listeners with increasingly short attention spans keep their attention on the text. Michael Raiter, director of the Centre for Biblical Preaching agrees:

> Generally, people's attention span for listening to a series of propositions is quite short; after a few minutes you can tell that people's minds are wandering. Therefore, it is important at regular intervals to give an illustration.

---

our first linguistic experiences took shape, we (most of us) had the privilege of hearing stories 'told' or read to us. Stories expanded our horizons. Some of them puzzled us. Some of them amused us. Some of them frightened us. Some of them gave us cautionary wisdom about how to survive in the wider world. They educated us, gave us principles to live by. In short, they were our first introduction to extended (and organized) thought and the development of character. Logical argumentation came later—much later. So, when we tell a story in a sermon, we are tapping into the earliest, and probably most influential, forms of learning that our listeners (and we, ourselves) experienced." Arnold, "Protagonist Corner," 36.

23. "Contemporary audiences are just not wired for long, informative discourses. They need stories, examples, or imaginative illustrations to help convey the message." Carter, Duvall, and Hays, *Preaching God's Word*, 133.

24. "Illustrations are an excellent means for arousing the attention. Often they will happily serve this purpose in the introduction to the sermon, securing at the outset the interest of the audience. But perhaps they are in this respect even more serviceable in the progress of the discourse, particularly if the attention has been somewhat strained by argument or description, and begins to flag." Broadus, *A Treatise on the Preparation and Delivery of Sermons*, 227. "It has been clearly shown that listeners regularly practice selective inattention by taking 'mini-breaks' from intensive concentration. After these short 'aural rests,' listeners rejoin the monologue, but only if it's of interest to them. Stories provide doorways through which this reentry is made—they help recapture attention." Brown, *Transformational Preaching*, 239.

Indeed, once you begin to tell a story you see people's body language change: they look up, straighten in their seats and even lean forward. If you have lost them, then a story usually brings them back. Therefore, I usually do not go too long without a story.[25]

It is not enough for an illustration to be interesting; it must function to create interest in the text. While Spurgeon encouraged opening the window and letting fresh air in, he wanted the illustration to serve the text, not draw people away from it.[26] Just as we would never open a window during a hurricane, we should never choose an illustration that creates interest in itself but not the text. The illustration (or the people in it) does not become the focus of the audience's attention but fades into the background as the clearer understanding of the biblical truth emerges. The illustration must focus attention on the text, not on itself.

The light metaphor is also helpful here. The light must be on the text, not on the subject matter of the illustration, and not on the speaker. Yes, the illustration needs to be interesting, but only so it can help the audience members understand, apply, or experience the text, which means it must focus attention on the text.

As Lane writes, "Good illustrations lead the listener to focus on the truth being expressed, not its referent. It is all too easy for the referent to 'take over.' This is a real danger with personal

---

25. Raiter, "On Sermons," 94–95. "The average mind begins to wander after extensive and lengthy discourse. Good illustrations help refocus attention on the message." Akin, Curtis, and Rummage, *Engaging Exposition*, loc 3373.

26. "Spurgeon is well known for employing striking images and illustrations as servants of the text. But he was careful to avoid turning them into amusements that navigated away from the text." Nettles, "Charles Haddon Spurgeon: The Prince of Preachers," 120.

illustrations, powerful stories, and movie clips. Listeners enjoy and remember the illustration, but miss the truth being expressed."[27]

There is a consensus on this point. Illustrations should be interesting but should never steal the show. Pastor Michael Easley encourages the use of illustrations but warns that illustrations should not overpower the text or become the point;[28] professor Ramesh Richard acknowledges that they should have entertainment value but should not become the focus of the sermon;[29] and communications professor Rosalie de Rosset warns against an illustration upstaging the text.[30]

There is an inherent danger of this happening with the use of media clips. Pastor Kevin Bergeson comments:

> Worship leaders now have access to an enormous collection of media, from local public libraries (seriously awesome) to the internet. But the very impact of that material might become the problem. Using a clip of leaping whales

---

27. Lane, "The God Who Illustrates," 337.

28. "Be careful not to let the illustration overpower the point or become the point. In other words, let the Bible guide your use of illustrations, rather than finding a great story and building the message around it." Easley, "Why Expository Preaching?," 34. See also Charette, "Keeping Your People Glued," 51: "We should deliver our illustrations with pathos, we should use vivid illustrations that do not overpower the text, and we should illustrate the propositional truth found in the text, but by all means we must temper our sermons with well-delivered illustrations."

29. "They make the material understandable, but they should not be the focal point of your sermon. Illustrations are not used to entertain (though they may have some entertainment value), but they are to help the audience understand the content or the claims of what is being illustrated." Richard, *Scripture Sculpture,* 125.

30. "Illustration well used never upstages the teaching of Scripture; instead, it brings its message home concretely and eloquently, gripping the heart and enlarging the understanding." de Rosset, "Felling the Devil," 238.

may be a powerful way to illustrate a creation story (see BBC's *Earth*), but what happens when people leave worship remembering only the whales and not the God who created the whales? Before simply firing up the DVD player in church, press "pause" and consider,[31]

The form of the illustration—electronic media—does not necessarily disqualify its use, but before deciding to use a video clip, it is wise to consider the possibility that its use might actually distract the congregation from the text[32] instead of creating interest in the text.[33] Some interesting illustrations call attention to themselves or the preacher, but do not call attention to the text. It could be because they are inappropriate or because they overpower the exegesis and replace the text as the focus of the sermon.[34]

It would be easy to evaluate how interesting an illustration is based solely on the amount of interest it generates, but that could be counterproductive to the sermon's purpose. The interest is only helpful if the illustration generates interest in the message. In evaluating how interesting an illustration is, you can use the following guide:

---

31. Bergeson, "Sanctuary as Cinema," 303.

32. "Illustrations should never distract or alienate people from the true message of God's Word." Farmer, "What Sermon Illustrations Should Be Banned?," 31.

33. "Stories and illustrations are only meant to illustrate truth, not to call attention to themselves." Lloyd-Jones, *Preaching and Preachers*, 244.

34. "While it is certainly not wrong for a preacher to utilize information from outside the Bible to support, illustrate, or apply the truth of God's Word, a line is crossed when the observations and assertions of some other preacher, psychologist, researcher, or futurist become the primary content of sermons." Shaddix, *The Passion Driven Sermon*, 38.

Red light	Yellow light	Green light
It is **probable** that the illustration will upstage the text.	It is **possible** that the illustration will upstage the text.	The illustration is **likely** to stimulate interest in the text.

Effective Illustrations Are Appropriate

The light metaphor is helpful to understand this characteristic. While illustrations should shine a light on the biblical truth, they should never shine a light into the listeners' eyes, blinding them to the text, which is exactly what inappropriate illustrations do.

It is possible that you could give a green light to each of the first three characteristics of effective illustrations (familiar, clear, and interesting) and yet choose not to use it because it is not appropriate. For instance, some preachers, in the name of creating interest, will be provocateurs, showing movie clips with questionable content[35] or using foul language. Maybe they want to signal that they are "keeping it real" or in tune with current culture. Neither takes priority over the text. For the illustration to work, it needs to call attention to the text, not itself. It is not appropriate to use coarse, vulgar, or shocking illustrations in a sermon.

Raiter writes, "One needs to be careful of illustrations that, while thoroughly engaging, are too shocking. If a very clever illustration is so graphic, so horrific, that some people switch off immediately, the risk is they will hear nothing else."[36] Some illustrations would not be offensive to anyone yet are still not appropriate to use.

---

35. For an example, see Wilson, *Future Church*, 137–38.
36. Raiter, "On Sermons and Preaching," 96.

Secondary audiences. Today, many churches livestream their sermons online so others can benefit from their pastors' messages. This kind of secondary audience could be larger than the one gathered in person, and not all the virtual audience members are listening with an open, understanding heart. Lane addresses this issue well:

> The freshest illustrations will arise from personal experience. Personal illustrations can also model the integration of the text with our own lives. However, preachers need to ensure that it is not they who become the focus, but God! Wisdom, perspective and balance are required here. An honest and transparent preacher is usually much appreciated by a congregation, as maturity and a healthy self-understanding in Christ is modeled. This sets a tone in a Christian community and helps build a healthy community. Nonetheless, there are appropriate limits to expressing honesty and transparency. Be careful not to feed an unhealthy voyeurism or curiosity unintentionally. The goal of the sermon has to be kept in mind. Will what is said be helpful, both in the present and in the longer-term? A sermon is a public address. With current technology it can be simultaneously available around the world and recorded for posterity. This new availability of sermons means that preachers now have to bear in mind a global audience who will be listening in very different contexts, geographically, temporally and culturally. When you share personal illustrations, listeners will think they know you. Some listeners will make assumptions based on the information you give that may be unhelpful for one's ongoing ministry. Not to mention the life of the congregation or the wider Christian community.[37]

---

37. Lane, "The God Who Illustrates," 341–42.

Even when preachers are speaking to a homogeneous congregation of people who they think share their viewpoints and values, if their church streams the sermon, that is no longer the case. This secondary audience may not be sympathetic to the pastor or the church. Political organizations with their own agendas may be viewing those sermons trolling for evidence that your church is a hate organization or looking for means to embarrass the pastor. Self-disclosure and transparency among an intimate community of believers is one thing, but once the church streams its services to the world, it is another.

Confidentiality and ethical considerations. In chapter 4, I will cover these considerations in depth as they relate to personal illustrations, but for now, let me simply mention that preachers should secure permission to use illustrations that involve other people, and when preachers say something happened to them, it should have actually happened.

In evaluating how appropriate an illustration is, you can use the following guide:

Red light	Yellow light	Green light
It is **probable** that someone in the primary or secondary audience will be offended or that the story breaks confidences.	It is **possible** that someone in the primary or secondary audience will be offended.	The illustration is **not likely** to offend members of the primary or secondary audience. The story does not break confidences.

In general, the sermon illustration evaluation rubric presented in this chapter will assist preachers in determining the potential effectiveness of a sermon illustration. However, not every sermon illustration will work in every part of the sermon. The next chapter gives special attention to the different roles of illustrations located in different parts of the sermon and in different sermon structures.

3

Illustration Location and Sermon Structure

The four metaphors (bridge, window, light, and picture) enhance our understanding of how sermon illustrations function to break down communication barriers and help preachers with their goal of meaning transmission. The four characteristics (familiarity, clarity, interest, and appropriateness) provide an evaluative framework for increasing the likelihood that the illustrations will be effective in communicating biblical truth. After understanding how sermon illustrations function in a sermon and what makes them effective, it is important to explore how they function in the different sections of the sermon (introduction, body, and conclusion) and in different sermon structures (deductive and inductive).[1]

In the simplest of terms, sermons have three sections: the beginning, the middle, and the end. Sermon illustrations at the beginning and the end of a sermon have a unique function because they do more than help others understand, apply, or experience a biblical truth. While certainly doing those things, they

---

1. For more information on sermon structures, see Wilson et al., *Impact Preaching*, chapter 2.

might also function to establish a connection, stimulate interest, or capture the essence of the teaching.

Deductive Sermon Structures

Deductive sermon structures like expositional (verse-by-verse) and multipoint sermons begin with a thesis or big idea and move through the body to a concluding call to action. Illustrations function differently in the body of the sermon than at the beginning or end. Because the big idea comes at the beginning, illustrations function to create interest in the big idea at the outset. Since the big application comes at the end, illustrations work to assist the listeners in experiencing or visualizing the big application. Both are exceedingly important.[2] Illustrations in the beginning help stimulate interest in the big idea, while illustrations at the end help motivate the listeners to be doers and not just hearers of the word (Jas 1:22).

In the body of the sermon, illustrations function to expand the listeners' attention span as they assist them in understanding, applying, or experiencing the biblical truth. Because illustrations function differently in the beginning, middle, and end, it is possible that an illustration that you have green-lighted on all four characteristics (familiar, clear, interesting, and appropriate) would work well in one part of the sermon but not another.

Introduction. In expositional or multipoint sermons, the introduction will usually include these three essential elements:

2. "Since form follows function, the structure of the sermon should dictate the place of our illustrations, but illustrations usually fit at certain places in the sermon. The most important places for illustrations are in the introduction and the conclusion. Nothing arouses audience interest or drives home the message of the sermon like a well-placed illustration to begin or to conclude the sermon. Nothing can open people up emotionally to receive difficult truth like a good illustration or story." York and Decker, *Preaching with Bold Assurance,* 153.

- *Establish a connection* between preacher and congregation.

- *Create interest* in the subject or text.

- *Orient the listener* by providing necessary background to locate the context, culture, and customs. The preacher may also use the *introduction* to announce the sermon thesis or provide a roadmap of the sermon's direction.

Preachers usually select illustrations for the introduction that do more than help listeners understand, apply, or experience the biblical truth. While they may function in that way, they also may need to establish a connection, stimulate interest, or orient the listener.[3]

Connect. Preachers either connect or reconnect with the congregation at the beginning of the sermon. If they are one of the primary preaching pastors of the church and have an ongoing relationship with the congregation, then it can be as simple as saying good morning or making a comment about church life. Often, they connect by praying a meaningful pastoral prayer that focuses on the needs of members of the congregation or on the church's mission. Regardless, there is usually a time of reconnecting.

However, the need to connect is more profound for preachers who are new to the congregation. Usually, gracious comments or

---

3. Hamilton, *Homiletical Handbook*, 53–54. Hamilton's list is longer than mine. He says there are five functions of the introduction: "1. Arouse interest. 2. It must inform the audience of the subject. 3. It shows the hearers their need to listen to the development of this particular subject (personal relevance). 4. It should promote the respect of the audience toward the speaker (ethos). 5. It should give some indication as to how the sermon is going to be developed."

a few words of personal introduction are helpful to put congregation members at ease.

Connection is not just about becoming acquainted or reacquainted, though. Sometimes, the connection is not just between the preacher and the people but also between the preacher and the subject. One of the ways preachers can effectively connect with the congregation is via a personal illustration that serves the dual purpose of introducing themselves and the subject to the audience. Chapter 4 includes a discussion on the pros and cons of using personal illustrations during a sermon's introduction, but if preachers can avoid "splitting the focus" and are able to include themselves among those needing the gospel without drawing attention away from the message, then a personal illustration can be an effective way to introduce a sermon.

In his sermon "Elijah—Unrealistic Expectations (1 Kings 19)," pastor Pat Damiani uses a personal illustration combined with a hypothetical illustration to introduce his sermon.

Fourteen years ago, I was a struggling bi-vocational church planter. Because our church plant had gone through some tough times, we were meeting at our house over the summer and praying for God's direction. During that time, I got a phone call from Denny Howard, who was the pastor here at TFC, asking if we would be willing to consider merging our church plant with Thornydale.

After Mary and I met with Denny and Anita, we decided we'd give it a test run. Thornydale already had plans to go through the *40 Days of Purpose* program, so we decided that our two groups would jointly participate in that program and then see what God would lead us to do from there.

Since our church plant had saved some funds, we decided that we would use those funds to send out a mass mailing of thousands of postcards to our community. The company that we used to assist us in that process assured us that we could expect a certain percentage of the people who received those postcards to respond by visiting the church, so we were really excited about the possibility that we could see dozens or even hundreds of visitors over the next few weeks after the mailing.

To our great disappointment, those expectations weren't even close to being met. I can't remember the exact numbers, but I don't think we had more than a handful of families who ended up visiting as a result of the mailing.

Over the years, we've attempted a few other big events or programs that we had very high hopes for, only to face similar disappointments.

And I suspect, based on my conversations with other pastors, disappointment is one of the regular hazards of being a pastor. Many times, I think we're our own worst critics; we get home on Sunday afternoon wondering if all the work we did during the week to prepare and deliver our message actually made any difference whatsoever, since we rarely get to see concrete results.

But I know that pastors aren't the only ones who experience that kind of disappointment. I think to some degree or another, every single person, and even every single disciple of Jesus, is prone to wonder if living a life of obedience to Jesus is really worth it. Perhaps on more than one occasion you've said something like this:

- I've tried to be the very best employee that I can be and work as if working for the Lord and not for men, but I haven't gotten a raise or a promotion in a long time.

- We've tried the very best we can to make Jesus the center of our marriage, but we still fight and argue from time to time.

- We've done our best to raise our kids to love Jesus, but they have still rebelled and are far away from God right now.

- We've tried to apply biblical principles with our finances, but we still struggle to pay our bills every month.

- I've prayed for and shared the gospel with a family member or friend, but they don't seem to want anything to do with Jesus.

Any of those sound familiar? If not, then congratulations. But for the rest of us, this morning's message is really important if we want to learn how to deal biblically with our disappointment.[4]

Damiani's illustration not only provides some personal background material, introducing himself to those in the congregation who were not familiar with him; it also shows him to be a fellow struggler, on the journey with everyone else—a person who struggles with unmet (unrealistic) expectations. To include the members of the congregation, he pivots from the personal story to using a hypothetical illustration containing a series of hypothetical situations, showing that the subject matter is not just for

4. Pat Damiani, "Elijah—Unrealistic Expectations," https://sermons.faithlife.com/sermons/200972-elijah-unrealistic-expecataions.

him or other pastors who experience deep disappointment but this is a common human experience. The hypothetical situations move attention away from his personal experience, broadening it into a shared human experience, demonstrating the relevance of the text to the people's current reality, and by doing so, they fulfill the next element in the introduction: create interest in the topic or text.

Create interest. Personal illustrations are one way to create interest in a text or topic, but other types of illustrations work well also. A fresh illustration from the opening scene of the movie *Courageous* works well as the introduction to a sermon on Hebrews 12:14–17:

> The movie *Courageous* begins with a young man at a gas station pulling the squeegee out of the water container so he can wash his windshield while he is filling up his tank. What he doesn't know is that a young stranger is about to steal his pickup.
>
> When he turns around, he sees the truck pulling away. He drops the squeegee and runs after it. He lunges through the pickup window and grabs on to the steering wheel. With his body halfway out of the truck and, at times, his feet dragging on the side of the street, the man refuses to let go of the wheel.
>
> At first, it seems strange that this man would hold on to the steering wheel with half of his body hanging out of the pickup. Viewers want to scream out, "It's not worth it—it is just a truck! File an insurance claim and move on." The truck runs into a tree, and the thief runs away. The owner opens the door, and the viewers see for the first time why he was in hot pursuit: it wasn't his truck he was

running after; it was his child. There was a young baby in
the car seat crying.

Some things are worth pursuing.

With the same determination—the determination of a
hot pursuit—we are to pursue peace and holiness.[5]

Members of the congregation who have seen the movie
Courageous will especially relate to the illustration, but even those
who have not seen the film will relate to doing whatever is necessary to protect a child and be better prepared for understanding
the intensity of the word "pursue."

I suppose another way to introduce the sermon would be to
mention that the Greek word translated as "pursue" is *diōkete*,
which is a present, active, imperative, second-person, plural verb
that means "to set in rapid motion" and is translated elsewhere in
the New Testament as "to persecute," and therefore, it is a word
that carries both urgency and intensity. However, a good illustrator
will find a way to capture the meaning, urgency, and intensity of
the word and present it with something that is familiar, clear, interesting, and appropriate. While parsing a Greek verb would work
to orient the listener (the next essential element of the introduction), it would not create interest in the same way this illustration
would. As fascinating as the discovery of nuance from the Greek
language is to a preacher while preparing a sermon, a Greek lesson
does not usually stimulate interest in a sermon, and if it belongs in
the sermon at all, it usually does not work well in the introduction.

Remember, the only time in the sermon that the preacher
has the congregation's full attention is during the introduction.
Wise preachers do not squander the congregation's initial listening

---

5.   Jim L. Wilson, "Are You in Pursuit of Peace and Holiness?," https://
sermons.faithlife.com/sermons/80031-are-you-in-pursuit-of-peace-and-holiness.

intensity with inaccessible content like a Greek lesson. Neither should they indulge in frivolity or minutiae; instead, effective preachers harness the people's undivided attention to convince them that this sermon will be worth their time. Homiletics professor Marvin McMickle writes, "Every effort must be made at the beginning of the sermon to make the case for why people should pay attention to what is going to follow."[6]

Orient the listener. The next essential feature of a good sermon introduction is that it orients the listener to what is happening in the text and what will be happening in the sermon; it provides a roadmap, acknowledging where we are, showing where we are going, and, perhaps, indicating how we will get there. In his sermon "The Way, Truth, and Life (John 14:6)," Derek Geldart orients his listeners with the following introduction:

> Can you imagine what it must have been like to be one of the disciples and hear the final words of Christ? After having witnessed Jesus walk on water, heal the sick, and bring the dead back to life, the disciples were unlikely ready to hear what Jesus was about to do next! On his way to Jerusalem, Jesus told the disciples that he was about to be delivered to the chief priests and teachers of the law, who would condemn and hand him over to the gentiles to be mocked, flogged, and crucified (Matt 20:17–19). After the Last Supper, Jesus told the disciples that once he was raised from the dead, he would remain with them but a short time and would then return to the right hand of God the Father in heaven (John 14:1–4). Peter's response to Jesus's predicted departure—wanting to die to return with him—and Philip's response of wanting to see God the

---

6. McMickle, *Shaping the Claim*, 38.

Father immediately are reactions we can understand and even empathize with. However, it is Thomas' response—"We don't know where you are going, so how can we know the way (14:5)?"—that has puzzled humanity for generations. In today's sermon, we are going to explore what Jesus meant when he told Thomas, "I am the way, the truth, and the life (14:6)."[7]

Geldart orients his listeners by setting the sermon's text in context with the recent events in the life of the disciples and asking the congregation to imagine what it would have been like to be an eyewitness to the recent events.[8]

Body. While there is no unimportant part of the sermon, the body is where the real meat is—it is the portion of the sermon where the Bible is taught and the weightier content occurs.[9] Certainly, not every verse or point needs an illustration, but the basic rhythm is read, explain, demonstrate, and apply. Read the text, explain what it means, demonstrate how it works, and then apply it to the lives of the congregation members.

---

7. Derek Geldart, "The Way, Truth, and Life (John 14:6)," https://sermons.faithlife.com/sermons/253467-the-way-truth-and-life.

8. For the research we did on the frequency of different types of sermon illustrations (see section 2), we defined a biblical illustration as an illustration that "summarizes a story or event from the Bible." While this introduction does not meet the criteria we set for a biblical Illustration, it does essentially function as one. The distinction is that it uses not a single story or event but a series of Bible events as a collective experience to form a single illustration.

9. "The body of your sermon, where the meat is given to the congregation, is the most important part; however, from a communications standpoint, an illustration at both ends of a sermon can make a difference. In the beginning it can prompt a congregation to listen, and in the end it can cause them to remember what they have heard." Brown, "Illustrating the Sermon," 204.

Most of this chapter is devoted to using illustrations at the beginning and end of the sermon, but that does not mean those in the middle are less important. The content is weighted toward those at the beginning and end because those in the middle conform to the norms established in the first two chapters of the book. The illustrations at the beginning and end are the ones that require special treatment.

The window metaphor (chapter 1) underscores the importance of sprinkling the biblical exposition with illustrations—letting some fresh air into the sermon. Because the human mind resists engaging in deep concentration for lengthy periods, sermon illustrations help break up the intense exegetical work so the congregation can engage the text for longer. However, the use of unrelated illustrations just for comic relief or a break could backfire. It could take attention away from the text and become an off-ramp into daydreaming. The illustration needs to be on point—it needs to relate to the subject. Remember, to get a green light, an illustration must create interest in the text, not just be interesting (chapter 2).

Illustrations in the body of the sermon increase listening capacity. They also help make the unfamiliar more understandable and help clarify what is obscure or foggy.

Conclusion. There are two essential elements of the sermon's conclusion: a big application of the sermon's "big idea" to life and a call for a commitment to action—to be doers of the word. Sermon illustrations can help with both of these essential elements. Pastor Brian Harbour puts it this way:

> Another effective way to conclude a sermon is with an illustration or story. The concluding story will flesh out and paint a portrait of the central theme of the sermon or its main points. ... An effective illustration will enable

us to see the truth discussed in the sermon. An effective illustration will also enable us to see our own life as it compares with the truth discussed in the sermon. In either case, the illustration or story will imprint the message on the listener's mind.[10]

Those who preach for transformation want the members of their congregation to respond to what they've learned about God in the sermon with a response that pleases God, with a mind that has been renewed by the word and not conformed to the ways of the world (Rom 12:1–2).[11] The ultimate goal is for the members of the congregation not just to understand the preacher's words but to live them out—to apply the message to their lives. After understanding comes application.

Sermon illustrations can assist in promoting transformation if they demonstrate how to apply the biblical principles or help the people experience what they have come to understand.

In my sermon "Do Not Love the World," based on 1 John 2:15–17, I conclude with an illustration from *The Lion King* of how God rescues us from temptation when we quote Scripture.

In the movie *The Lion King*, Simba, the baby lion, takes his friend Nala to the Elephant Graveyard. Although this was strictly forbidden by his father, Simba laughs in the face of danger to impress his friend. Once there, they are chased by the dangerous hyenas and eventually get cornered. In desperation, Simba tries to roar at the hyenas, but only a laughable growl of a baby lion comes out. As the hyenas are encroaching on them, they taunt Simba to try again. This time, Simba takes a step back and gets ready

---

10.   Harbour, "Concluding the Sermon," 219.

11.   Wilson et al., *Impact Preaching,* chapter 3.

to roar again with all his might. To the viewers' surprise, the thunderous roar of a full-grown male lion bursts out into the theater. Mufasa, Simba's father, has roared in the background.

If you attempt to resist Satan on your own, you might experience the sense of helplessness that Simba did, but when you quote Scripture, you are not facing temptation alone. When you open your mouth, the roar from the Lion from the tribe of Judah fills the air—and Satan turns and runs.[12]

Inductive Sermon Structures

Inductive sermon structures (one-point and narrative sermons) require fewer illustrations than deductive structures do. Because narratives tend to captivate an audience and hold their attention, narrative sermons based on narrative passages may require fewer illustrations than deductive sermons. Greidanus writes, "If one uses the narrative form for preaching Hebrew narratives, few illustrations will be required to clarify and carry the message since the narrative form itself performs that function."[13]

Notice that Greidanus qualifies the use of the narrative form for preaching narrative passages. When I wrote *How to Write Narrative Sermons,* I allowed for using the narrative sermon form for almost any text. I have changed my view since then. In my most recent homiletics book, which I coauthored with three biblical scholars, we took the view that the narrative sermon form is not always appropriate and should be reserved for literary forms that make a single point.[14] This observation is not an argument

---

12. Jim L. Wilson, "Do Not Love the World (1 John 2:15–17)," https://sermons.faithlife.com/sermons/486962-do-not-love-the-world.

13. Greidanus, *The Modern Preacher and the Ancient Text*, 227.

14. Wilson et al., *Impact Preaching.*

for abandoning deductive sermon forms but simply underscores the wisdom of keeping the full impact of the text intact by choosing the sermon form based on its literary form. Moreover, if the form is narrative, it likely will need fewer illustrations for sustaining interest.

However, that does not mean that inductive sermons never use illustrations. Hamilton maintains, "Good illustrations will enhance the effect of inductive sermons. With some inductive approaches, the main points are based on ancient examples with which the hearer may not readily identify. Contemporary illustrations and applications can bridge this time gap."[15] One of the best ways to utilize illustrations in an inductive sermon is to weave the illustration into the sermon plot dynamic that arises from the text. Most of the examples in this book include an illustration with a citation to the full sermon so you can see the illustration in the full context of the sermon. In the following case, I am providing the full text of a sermon on Luke 1:13 since it is necessary to read the entire sermon to see how the personal illustration is woven into the sermon and how it relates to the text.

> Elizabeth had long since resigned herself to the fact that she would never hear the patter of little feet in the home where she and her husband, Zechariah, lived. Elizabeth was barren. "Barren"—the very word elicits thoughts of sand blowing across a desert wasteland.
>
> Zechariah was in the sanctuary carrying out his priestly duties when God interrupted him. Gabriel, the angel that stands in the very presence of God, left his coveted place to stand in the presence of God's priest. Shocked by the angelic sight, Zechariah became frightened. Zechariah

---

15. Hamilton, *Homiletical Handbook*, 101.

wasn't expecting to hear a word from the Lord while he was doing his religious duty.

Gabriel had some good news: "But the angel said to him, 'Do not be afraid, Zacharias, for your petition has been heard, and your wife Elizabeth will bear you a son, and you will give him the name John' " (Luke 1:13 NASB).

"Your prayer has been heard"--what prayer! Likely, Zechariah hadn't done any praying for a child in years. He'd forgotten about the prayer, but God hadn't. In his perfect timing, God answered a young man's prayer when he was too old to remember it and gave his wife a son when she was too old to conceive on her own.

How could a religious man be surprised to find a word from God in the sanctuary? Why would a priest doubt that God could answer his stale prayer?

Even spiritual men have moments when their faith flickers. Let me explain what I mean.

When the angel of the Lord told him he would have a son, Zechariah doubted the prophecy. It is impossible, Zechariah thought, for an old man and a barren woman to have a son. After fifty-plus years of disappointment, perhaps I'd doubt too. How about you?

After he expressed his doubt, Zechariah was speechless.

Literally, Zechariah was speechless. "And now, since you didn't believe what I said, you won't be able to speak until the child is born. For my words will certainly come true at the proper time" (Luke 1:20 NLT).

I don't know what constitutes the greater miracle—an elderly woman having a baby or a preacher being quiet for nine months. Though I have no experience having a baby, I did have a time in my life when I couldn't speak. It was a humbling experience.

During a surgery to remove a cancerous thyroid, the doctor tapped on my recurrent laryngeal nerve, thinking it was fatty tissue. The assistant surgeon assured the doctor it was not the nerve and advised that he cut it. Twice he asked for an instrument to sever the structure, but when he tried, his hand froze. "Because I tapped on the nerve," the doctor explained to me, "it no longer transmits the signal from the brain to the vocal cord." The result was a paralyzed vocal cord.

"But doctor," I whispered, "I'm a preacher; what do I do without a voice?"

I stared into my doctor's eyes. "Will my voice come back?" He blinked and looked away. "I don't know, maybe, since I didn't cut the nerve. Normal function could return in a few months, or it could be permanent."

In that moment, faced with an impossible situation, my theology and this unfortunate reality rammed together full force in a head-on collision. In that moment, I had more questions than answers. Will I ever preach again? How will I earn a living? What about my family? WHERE ARE YOU, GOD?

Like Zechariah, I doubted.

That night, I lay in bed as a thick silence surrounded me. "God, I'm over here," I prayed. "Are you watching? Why are you doing this to me? Why don't you heal me?"

God's people were good to me. The church supported me, and preachers from our state convention office in Albuquerque filled my pulpit as I waited for my healing.

My wife and my mother were my greatest encouragers throughout the ordeal; they pumped me with hope and calmed me when I had soul seizures. I worried about paying the bills, about the welfare of the church, and about our future. Susan never worried. "Everything is going to be fine," she'd say. "God will take care of us." Her strength buttressed my crumbling faith. "God will heal you," my mother said; "He wouldn't call you to preach without supplying you a voice." These words were my lifeline. I held to them like a drowning man.

Clearly, God's hand kept the surgeon from cutting the nerve, and I fully expected to get my voice back. Every morning when I awoke, I said, "I love you, Susan." When the words came out in a whisper instead of a normal voice, I swallowed and thought, tomorrow—tomorrow will be the day. My miracle will come.

Tomorrow never came. I was confused the day I checked into the hospital for additional surgery to correct the problem. God where are you, and why didn't you heal me?

Immediately after the surgery, my voice was strong, but after the swelling went down, I had a coarse, breathy voice that projected slightly above a whisper. With every tick of the clock, it got weaker, and I grew more confused. Though the congregation encouraged me, I knew I was no longer a good preacher. My voice was too weak.

The disability had its accompanying trials. Drive-through windows were the absolute worst. On one occasion, the operator mocked my breathy whisper when he took my order. His immaturity brought out my own; I wanted to squash him like a bug.

The only time I cried through the ordeal happened about a month after I lost my voice. I stood next to the guest preacher as we began to sing: "I love you Lord, and I lift my voice …" Of course, I didn't try to sing—it hurt too bad to force the wind. I just mouthed the words. But when I got to the word "voice," I began to cry. "What good am I to you, Lord?" I prayed. "I can't even worship with your people."

Occasionally, I got a chuckle out of my disability. I wrote the name of a person I wanted to visit on my notepad and showed it to a hospital volunteer to get a room number. The kind woman slanted her head and asked, "Can you hear me?" Of course, I could hear, but I couldn't speak to tell her; I had to write "yes" on the pad.

Notice that Zechariah's friends did the same thing when Elizabeth followed the angel's instructions to name her baby "John."

"'What?' they exclaimed. 'There is no one in all your family by that name.' So they asked the baby's father, communicating to him by making gestures. He motioned for a writing tablet, and to everyone's surprise he wrote, 'His name is John!' Instantly Zechariah could speak again, and he began praising God" (Luke 1:61–64 NLT).

Did he praise God because he could speak, or did he speak because he could praise God? This isn't a chicken-or-egg type of question. Think about it. A man communicating with a pencil and tablet doesn't even try to speak. His praise erupted. Praise burst through his sealed lips and flowed to the glory of God.

Like Zechariah, my voice is back. After a third surgery, I have a near-normal voice. Though I thanked God for giving Dr. Netterville the skill to heal me, I still wondered why God didn't intervene. That is, until a comment the doctor made during a follow-up visit. "Your nerve is transmitting enough signal that the vocal cord is staying healthy—not enough that it can ever move again, but enough to give a rich sound when supported by the silicone implant."

"Dr. Netterville," I asked, "what would my voice have been like if the surgeon had cut the nerve instead of tapping it?" I heard his voice and God's at the same time. He said, "Your voice would have always sounded hoarse." God said, "See, you got your miracle after all."

Because he is faithful, you can trust in God, even while you wait on his response to your need.

This side of my miracle, I view life a little differently. I praise God that though my faith may flicker from time to time, it never fails! Zechariah probably had the same thought when he bounced his newborn baby prophet on his knee.[16]

Notice how this sermon feathers the essential elements of the introduction naturally into the body of the sermon. There is not a sense of leaving the introduction to move into the body, especially since the sermon's first movement essentially was the introduction. A narrative sermon structure has movements, not points.[17] The first movement introduces the problem, creating

---

16. Jim L. Wilson, "Like the Birth of John to Aging Parents, God Does His Work in His Time," https://sermons.faithlife.com/sermons/80073-like-the -birth-of-john-to-aging-parents-god-does-his-work-in-his-time. This sermon has also been published in Wilson et al., *Impact Preaching*, 160–63.

17. For more information on sermon movements, see Wilson et al., *Impact Preaching*, chapter 2: (1) introduction of the problem, (2) attempt to resolve the problem, (3) failure to resolve the problem, and (4) resolution of the problem. See also Lowry, *Homiletical Plot*. Lowry sees the plot as having five movements: (1) upsetting the equilibrium, (2) analyzing the discrepancy, (3) disclosing the clue to the resolution, (4) experiencing the gospel, and (5) anticipating the consequences.

interest with the inherent tension. Technically, the first movement is not an introduction; it is part of the sermon's body.

The other elements of the introduction—orient the listener and connect with the congregation—naturally fold into the sermon's movements. Because the listeners have grown up listening to stories in their homes, churches, and schools, they do not need an orientation—they know the dynamics of a narrative-based discourse. In addition, instead of providing background material in the introduction, preachers can give it on an as-needed basis in the narrative.

While some inductive sermons will need a preliminary moment to connect at the beginning, because this one has a personal illustration woven into the body, it does not need one. The connection occurs in the body of the sermon as the personal story unfolds along with the biblical story. An interesting thing happens with this sermon structure: people automatically will weave their own story into the fabric of the sermon. They hear both the biblical story and the preacher's personal story, and they insert their own.

This sermon structure has the essential elements of both the introduction and the conclusion in the body. The big application and the call to action occur in the fourth movement, which resolves the problem. In this sermon, it is this statement: "Because he is faithful, you can trust in God, even while you wait on his response to your need."

While all illustrations must be familiar, clear, interesting, and appropriate to be effective, those that occur at the beginning and end of a sermon may need to do more than assist the audience in understanding, applying, or experiencing the biblical teaching. In deductive sermons, they take on the characteristics of their location. In the introduction, they function to create a connection or stimulate interest in the message; at the end, they serve to capture the essence of the teaching and provide a call to action.

Inductive sermon structures, like a narrative sermon on a narrative passage, do not require as many illustrations as deductive sermon forms. However, they can still use illustrations to overcome communication obstacles.

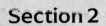

Section 2

Using a Variety of Illustration Types Well

4

Personal Illustrations

Preachers in our sample group used personal illustrations more than any other type of illustration (24 percent), narrowly surpassing fresh illustrations (22 percent) for the top spot.[1] The study confirmed what I have observed in the classroom: preachers are using personal stories in their sermons with great frequency.

Personal illustrations are an effective way to prepare the congregation to hear biblical truth. They can be interesting, down-to-earth, relatable, and helpful in creating a bond between the preacher and the congregation. Derek Geldart does a good job of using a personal illustration in his sermon "The Way, Truth, and Life." In the body of the sermon, he uses a story from his childhood to illustrate how the disciples could have been feeling when they heard that Jesus was going to be leaving them.

> I remember the very first time I went to a summer camp. As a young boy, I had never stayed away from home any more than a single night. One day at church, there was an announcement that the church was willing to sponsor children to go to Camp Wildwood. My parents asked

---

1. Because of the small sample size, this does not represent a statistically significant difference.

me if I wanted to go, and at first, I said, NO. After much coaxing and prodding, and with the promise that I could return whenever I wanted, with great reservations I finally said, YES. I remember that the trip from Hillsborough to the camp at McKees Mills seemed like it would take forever! When I arrived, my parents had to coax me to stay, for I was incredibly shy and did not make friends easily. The mere thought of being in a cabin with boys I did not know, being asked to participate in sporting events, singing, swimming, or eating food with others absolutely petrified me! The only thing that got me through that week was that I knew I could call at any time and my parents would come and get me. Knowing my way home helped me to endure and bear the loneliness of being separated from my parents.

Like me at camp, the disciples could only bear being separated from the Master If they knew how they could one day go and be with him. So, Jesus told them that the key to knowing and being with God the Father was not through our efforts to follow the law that was powerless because it was weakened by the flesh (Rom 8:3) but through belief in him who was the "way, the truth, and the life" (John 14:6).[2]

While the disciples were not children and were not being separated from their parents, there were enough parallels between Geldart's childhood experience and those in the biblical narrative to justify the use of the illustration. When he was a child, Geldart was emotionally dependent on his parents, just as the disciples

---

2. Derek Geldart, "The Way, Truth, and Life," https://sermons.faithlife.com/sermons/253467-the-way-truth-and-life.

were dependent on Jesus. In both cases, there was a separation from a beloved and respected authority figure.

However, what makes the illustration work is not how closely the relationships align but the frame of mind the story creates in the hearers. The illustration helps them experience a bit of the disciples' vulnerability through the shared childhood experience of being separated from parents for the first time. In speaking of his shyness and loneliness as a child, Geldart creates a connection between himself and his audience, but he also helps the congregation members relate to the disciples. The illustration becomes a bridge to a better understanding of what the disciples were experiencing by relating the familiar (separation from parents) with the unfamiliar (the disciples' separation from Jesus).

It's possible that Geldart could have accomplished the same goal with a hypothetical illustration; for instance, "What thoughts go through a child's mind when dropped off at summer camp for the first time?" Or, "I wonder if the disciples felt like a child spending extended time away from her parents for the first time." Or he could take a completely different approach to help the audience relate to generalized fear. He could have used a fresh illustration like this one:

> Different pollsters ask people different questions about what they are afraid of. Putting some of the questions together, we discover that "42 percent are afraid of being a victim of a random mass shooting, up from 16 percent in 2015 (Chapman University), and 57 percent of teens worry about gunfire erupting at their schools (Pew Research). Washington gives much cause for concern: 74 percent are fearful of corrupt government officials (Chapman University), and 30 percent worry President Trump is being framed for crimes by the FBI and the

Justice Department (Economist/YouGov). Sixty-four percent fear that another world war will erupt in the next forty
years (YouGov). Like so many other issues the nation can't
agree on, we're also divided on which is scarier, sharks or
President Trump; 43 percent say sharks, and 42 percent,
Trump (Public Policy Polling)."[3]

All these alternatives adequately introduce the topic, but they
do not provide the same laser focus as his personal illustration.
The hypothetical illustrations are so open-ended that they could
take the audience members into multiple states of mind, and I
would red-light the fresh illustration on appropriateness because
it has so many hot-button topics—gun control, mass shootings,
politics—that it could backfire and take attention totally away
from the sermon. Besides, the fresh illustration could only be
effective if the congregation were homogeneous in its political
views. However, its effectiveness would be limited because of the
incongruent tone.

I would yellow-light the clarity characteristic of the fresh illustration because the negative emotions generated by the illustration
are not equivalent to what the disciples would likely be feeling. By
choosing to use this specific personal illustration, Geldart limits
the distractions that these other approaches would introduce and
prepares the members of the congregation to engage with the text.

Besides, the endearing story works on many levels. I wonder
if any young children in the crowd listened with greater intensity
because their pastor was speaking of a time when he was their
age. Were there any shy or insecure people in the audience that

3.   Jim L. Wilson and Rodger Russell, "What Are You
Afraid Of?," https://sermons.faithlife.com/sermons/352656-what
-are-you-afraid-of.

day who gained some strength knowing they were not the only ones who struggle?

Culturally, it makes sense to use personal illustrations. One of the ways preachers can leverage the current culture for the gospel's sake is to "get real," which includes being transparent and genuine in and out of the pulpit.[4] Authenticity is important. While there are some members of every congregation who want their preacher to be perfect, the majority understand that preachers, like other members of the human race, are flawed individuals and prefer them to preach out of an authentic, less-than-perfect ethos rather than out of a faux perfection.

In general, there is an expectation that preachers will share a bit of their lives when they preach.[5] This is not so the people will know more about the preacher but so they will have a model of what it looks like to be self-reflective (Rom 12:3).

Purely on a communication level, listening to honest self-disclosure encourages mutuality.[6] By design, it models the way for members of the congregation to be honest about their strengths, weaknesses, fears, and potential.

In our sample group, over 40 percent of the sermons had at least one personal illustration, and 10 percent had more than one. Most of the preachers and homileticians that we studied while researching this book would agree that personal illustrations are an effective way to illustrate biblical truth.

---

4. Wilson, *Future Church,* 97–128.

5. "Today's audiences expect the preacher to be personal and winsome. This means not only speaking to the personal needs of people, but also using illustrations out of the preacher's life experience." Robinson, "Bringing Yourself into the Pulpit," 130.

6. "The pastor's self-disclosure invites others to be honest with their lives." Chartier, *Preaching as Communication,* 34.

Some see self-disclosure and sharing personal illustrations as hallmarks of their preaching ministry. Craig Blomberg and John Huffman are two examples. Blomberg writes, "I like to disclose something of my own life in most of my messages."[7] And Huffman maintains, "A major feature of my preaching as well as pastoral style has been a self-revelatory expression, both in terms of identification with others and personal illustrations of the truth I am endeavoring to share."[8]

In fact, there is a chorus of preachers and homileticians who encourage the use of personal illustrations. Hershael York and Bert Decker say they are "great believers" in the use of personal illustrations:

> Probably nothing else we say about illustrations will be as debatable as this piece of advice, but we are great believers in using tasteful, appropriate personal illustrations. Other kinds of stories and anecdotes may work fine, but you will be amazed to discover that the people who give you their time every Sunday morning are most interested in your personal stories. They enjoy hearing about your struggles, your victories, and even your thoughts. They don't have to be stories of earth-shattering drama or personal crisis, just little insights that shed some light on the subject of the text.[9]

Provost Thomas Cornman says that they can draw attention to how God helps believers achieve their potential.[10] In Capill's

---

7. Blomberg, *Preaching the Parables,* 43.

8. Huffman, "The Role of Preaching in Ministry," 425.

9. York and Decker, *Preaching with Bold Assurance,* 166.

10. "The honest, unvarnished expression of our experiences can serve as powerful illustrations for the texts of the Bible. These personal histories, when

words, they "may bring a matter home to the heart";[11] Richard tells preachers, "Never apologize for personal illustrations";[12] and Raiter writes, "The more personal the illustration the better it will be."[13]

Use with Caution

While many encourage the use of personal illustrations, others are more cautious. Mark Galli's article titled "Enough of Me Already!: It's Time to Find Other Ways to Illustrate Sermons than Me, Me, and Mine," summarizes his position well. In it, he writes, "Phillips Brooks once described preaching as 'Truth through personality.' Indeed. But with the flowering of the personal illustration, preaching often morphs into 'the truth of my personality.' "[14]

Homiletics professor David Buttrick writes, "To be blunt, there are virtually no good reasons to talk about ourselves from the pulpit."[15] While Buttrick does not argue for a total ban of personal illustrations, he is especially leery of using them at the beginning of a sermon (as Stanley and Jones promote[16]) because

---

presented with a focus on the work of God may not make us larger than life in the minds of our congregants, but they should point them to the one who desires their best and has called upon us to help them in that quest." Cornman, "History: The Hidden Gold Mine," 264.

11. Capill, *Preaching with Spiritual Vigour*, 148.

12. Richard, *Scripture Sculpture,* 128.

13. Raiter, "On Sermons and Preaching," 96.

14. Galli, "Enough of Me Already," 89.

15. Buttrick, *Homiletic: Moves and Structures*, 142.

16. Stanley and Jones, *Communicating for a Change*, 47. Stanley and Jones recommend that sermons begin with "The ME section" because "an audience needs a certain comfort level with a speaker before they'll really listen."

of the danger of "split-focus."[17] Pastor Geoff Sinibaldo says that he uses personal illustrations, but he works at not splitting the focus by putting too much attention on his "personal heroism." He writes of "wrong hero sermons":

> These sermons are testimonials to human spiritual heroism. They are powerful, often recounting the struggles of faith of either the preacher or of someone else who came to faith. But the journey is misdirected when the person becomes the example of faith rather than announcing faith given in and through Jesus Christ. When I preach, it is true, I use a lot of personal stories. But any preacher who does so must be careful not to end up focusing on personal heroism but instead the opposite, focusing on Christ who gives forgiveness, life, and salvation.[18]

Richard agrees. Earlier, I included a partial quote from Richard. However, the fuller quote adds depth to this discussion. "Never apologize for personal illustrations," he writes, but he continues, "but try not to be the hero of the story every time."[19] Never apologize is only half of his message. He qualifies it with

---

17. "Introductions featuring material drawn from a preacher's personal experience seem to be a growing trend. Perhaps, the practice has been encouraged by 'Tell-your-own-story' theology. Nevertheless, though personal illustrations may, on rare occasions, be used in the body of a sermon, personal experiences in an introduction are devastating. The problem is split focus. As a preacher, you are attempting at the onset of a sermon to focus congregational consciousness on an image, or an idea, or a scriptural passage, or whatever. But, by speaking of yourself, inevitably the congregation will focus on you. There is no way to prevent the split. Personal narratives will always introduce a preacher, and the intended subject matter will not form in congregational consciousness in any satisfactory fashion." Buttrick, *Homiletic: Moves and Structures*, 94.

18. Sinibaldo, "Lousy Preaching," 31.

19. Richard, *Scripture Sculpture*, 128.

a strong statement that the personal illustration is not about you ultimately—you are not using it to hold yourself up as a hero to the congregation.

However, others demonstrate that it is possible to use a personal illustration in the sermon introduction without splitting the focus. John R. Weathersby effectively achieves this in his sermon "Jesus Is Better" with an illustration from his childhood:

> When I was a kid, there were things I had to be careful of. When I went outside to ride my bike, I was supposed to be careful, looking before I crossed the road. I remember a farmer stopping to sternly talk to me because I'd set up old tires and wood to make a launch ramp, but it was at the end of my blind driveway and led straight into the road. There was no fear.
>
> Also, we were on this hugely long driveway, and I had to take the trash cans down to the end of that dark driveway through the woods.
>
> I remember I would bravely, as bravely as I could, carry those cans down, but by the time I'd gotten to the end of that terrifying driveway, I sprinted with everything in my body because of the fear of the dark and unknown. Fear drove a real reaction in me.
>
> Today, we'll see God motivating us to real reaction, through fear.[20]

This introduction eased me into the subject; it did not compete with it or overpower it. I had no problem shifting from the preacher's experience back to the text.

---

20. John R. Weathersby, "Jesus Is Better," https://sermons.faithlife.com/sermons/254006-hebrews-jesus-is-better:-today-is-the-day.

Finding the Middle Ground

As with many issues, preferred practices are found not on either end of a spectrum but somewhere in the middle. Pastors and scholars Warren and David Wiersbe offer wise counsel about finding balance with this issue. They write, "Some preachers talk about themselves so much, you could reconstruct their lives from their sermons. Others are so private that their personal experiences are told as anonymous anecdotes. Both extremes should be avoided. The congregation wants to see Christ, but they want to see him through the ministry of a real person, even one who occasionally makes mistakes."[21]

How then do you decide whether it is appropriate to use personal illustrations? Certainly, the general guidelines in the first section of the book are applicable, but in addition to those thoughts, this particular type of illustration has some issues that distinguish it from the other seven types. Therefore, personal illustrations need to be.

- **Authentic**. They need to have really happened to the preacher.

- Communicated in an **ethical** manner. If the illustration involves others, their permission should be secured, and no boundaries should be violated or confidences broken.

- **Proportionate**. They should not be the only type of illustration used, and preachers should guard against them being about the same thing over and over.

---

21. Wiersbe and Wiersbe, *The Elements of Preaching*, 103–4.

- **Suitable**. Some stories are suitable for a public gathering of worship, and some are not.

Authentic

By definition, a personal illustration is a story based on the preacher's own experiences. It should have actually happened—it should come from the preacher's own experiences.[22] Otherwise, it fails to be authentic.

During my first year of college, two different chapel speakers told the same story as if it happened to them. The first time I heard the story, I was moved. The second time, I felt duped. Retelling a story that happened to someone else as if it happened to you will cause the congregation to see you as dishonest.[23] As Robinson writes, "Some speakers say that putting yourself into a story, whether you really were there or not, is legitimate. But it can also create distrust. I have heard several well-known preachers use anecdotes I've read in old illustration books. They tell them as though the experience happened to them. Their credibility is destroyed."[24]

---

22. "Credibility requires appropriate acknowledgement of borrowed material. This certainly does not deny the existence of commonplace topics and illustrations freely exchanged and used. The problem occurs when originality is claimed or when one presents the experience of another as one's own." Bailey, "Ethics in Preaching," 552.

23. "Never, NEVER relate as your own an illustration from the life of another person. It is dishonest and it could be embarrassing as well. Somebody listening might know the truth about the story." Wiersbe and Wiersbe, *The Elements of Preaching*, 86–87.

24. Robinson, "Raisins in the Oatmeal," 98.

More recently, I heard a story told in the context of the sermon as if it happened to the preacher. [25] As I read and later listened to the sermon, it did not have the "ring of truth" to it, so I searched online for some key words in the story and found it at a Christian joke website.[26] As the preacher told the story, he did not stick to the script; he embellished it a bit for maximum humorous impact. The audience had a good laugh. Because he told it in a tongue-in-cheek manner, it may be that everyone knew it really did not happen to him. From the audience's reaction on the audio recording, I suspect they were fine with the way he presented the story.

However, I do not see the upside of telling a fictional story as real. Why not simply introduce the joke by replacing "This once happened to me" with "I ran across a story the other day that I related to; perhaps you will too"? Or at the end, say, "Of course this really didn't happen to me, but I thought you'd enjoy the story." With this minor change, the evaluation of the illustration shifts from a yellow light to a green light for clarity.

Ethical Regarding Friends

Preachers are not the main character in every personal illustration. Sometimes, they are observers. In his sermon "The Valley Is a Temporary Place," Spencer Miller uses the following personal illustration about his good friend whom God transformed through difficult days:

> I have a dear friend who admittedly lived an extremely sinful life of alcohol, drugs, and sex with women other than his wife. He told me that his life was not complete

25.   Sonny Sellers, "Best Dressed," https://sermons.faithlife.com/sermons/203436-sunday-september-10-2017-9-am.

26.   "The New Suit," accessed September 1, 2021, http://jokes.ochristian.com/Fashion/The_New_Suit.shtml.

until he was involved in a serious automobile accident; prior to this, his life was miserable and headed for a sure disaster. His vehicle was totaled, but there was not one scratch on his body—he said that he took it as a warning that he was headed in the wrong direction in his life. For sure, no one wants to experience an accident of this nature, but this particular accident opened my good friend's eyes, and as the years passed by, I can report to you that this same man has a wonderful preaching ministry in El Paso, Texas today. He lived a wild life in the valley but received a gift from God while in the valley.[27]

This is a powerful story that happened in the preacher's presence but not to the preacher. In telling the story, he did not overly insert himself; he just told it as an observer. It was a relatable story. If his listeners had not been through a season of open sin themselves, they likely had family members who had. Like most personal illustrations, this one gets a green light for familiarity. Without telling how the story personally applies to the audience, the people could make an immediate application. This illustration does a good job of showing that the valley is used ultimately for God's purpose.

In this case, Miller uses a semi-public story—he was not telling his congregation anything that his friend had not told his own congregation. In my view, it was appropriate. However, most have heard preachers use personal illustrations from their pastoral relationships that are inappropriate. For instance, telling a story from a counseling session—even if it occurred at another church—is not wise. Preacher and author Fred Craddock cautions:

---

27. Spencer Miller, "The Valley is a Temporary Place," https://sermons.faithlife.com/sermons/122734-the-valley-is-a-temporary-place.

Can ministers use in sermons events or conversations from their pastoral work? The temptation to do so is often strong since the appropriateness of such material will be very evident. However, private is private and confidence is confidence. No one will speak in confidence to a minister if there is a chance the conversation will make next Sunday's sermon. In fact, parishioners will be cautious if the preacher shares confidences from a previous parish since they know they will appear in sermons in the next parish.[28]

These stories often cast the counselee as foolish, unreasonable, and needy and tend to make the pastor out to be wise, sage, and heroic. There can only be one hero in the sermon, and it should not be the pastor.[29] Pastors must take care in their illustrations not to promote themselves. Stuart Briscoe says it well:

Self-promotion also occurs when we use half-stories that make us look good because we tell only the good half, or when we name-drop. It also rears its ugly head when we appear always to have the right answer: "Somebody came to me with a problem, and I told him …" Too many

---

28. Craddock, *Preaching*, 207.

29. "The fact is that someone will be the hero of our sermon or Bible study: Do we want the hero to be us or Jesus?" Moseley, *From the Study to the Pulpit*, 200. "While it is good to have personal illustrations, and I think it is important for people to see 'the real you' in a sermon, a preacher must be so careful of regularly presenting himself/herself as the hero of every story. Few things are more off-putting than a vain, self-obsessed preacher. I have sat under such preachers and it is excruciating and, indeed, undermines anything else that is good that the preacher has to say. Much better is Paul's approach, which is to boast of your weaknesses. People will respond to your preaching if you talk more of your failures than of your successes. Still, be careful of talking too much about yourself." Raiter, "On Sermons and Preaching," 95–96.

of these illustrations come across as self-promotion. And that's not our business. Our task is God-promotion.[30]

Ethical Regarding Family

Should preachers use stories that involve their immediate family members? Rarely is a personal experience exclusively the preacher's personal experience. It often involves family members. Tony Merida cautions about using too many stories featuring family members,[31] while York and Decker encourage preachers to ask permission before doing so,[32] and Silas Krueger cautions against using stories that involve children as sermon illustrations.[33]

When my children were living in our home, I did use illustrations about them in my sermons. Recently, I asked one of my grown sons about how he felt about this. He said that sometimes he didn't mind, but other times it was a problem for him. Especially because his friends would tease him afterward. He wanted to blend in with his peers and not have the pastor call attention to him.

---

30. Briscoe, "The Subtle Temptations of Preaching," 149–50.

31. "A word of caution is to remember not to use too many family illustrations. Your family, especially your wife, will probably even thank you for ceasing to tell everything that happened in the previous week. Your family does not need to think that everything you do is going to end up in next week's sermon." Merida, *Faithful Preaching*, 109.

32. "And when it comes to illustrations about family, ask permission from any family member you will mention before you dare use it. Their answer will depend on their personality and their confidence in you, but if they say no, respect it and accept that answer. Do not let your family feel like they have no privacy or control of how their private lives are presented to the congregation. Let sanctified common sense guide your use of personal illustrations and you will find them worthwhile." York and Decker, *Preaching with Bold Assurance,* 167–68.

33. "I would like to offer a brief comment about the use of personal experiences or stories involving your family members: Don't!" Krueger, "Preaching in an Oral Age," 109–10.

I am a pastor's son. My father was an active preacher into his mid-eighties. Most of the time, like my son, I did not mind when Dad told a story about me. I did not mind it when I was living in his home and did not mind it so much as an adult. But one story that he told repeatedly bothered me. He told it when I was living in his home and long after I was on my own. Whenever I visited my parents after they retired, I would attend church wherever Dad was interim pastor. On many occasions, people from the various churches would ask me, "Are you the son who had the frog jump up his pant legs?" Being asked this was embarrassing to me, and I would prefer not to be known by that event.

From my point of view, the story does not belong to Dad. It is mine. Everyone has stories like it in their childhood, but only the preacher's kids have their stories aired in public. I now side with Krueger on this issue. Do not tell stories about your minor children—ever. Not even flattering stories. York and Decker are right about seeking consent from family members before telling their stories, but that does not cover the special circumstances of minor children. They do not have the capacity to consent because of the imbalance of power between parent and child. It is possible that they would say yes regardless of how they felt.

Proportionate

Because they can be effective, it is tempting for some preachers to use personal illustrations all the time. A problem arises, though, when they go to that well so often that they find themselves telling the same stories repeatedly. Before long, the congregation can lip-sync the story as the preacher is telling it. While some are lip-syncing, others are rolling their eyes.

The tendency to overuse the same story is especially prevalent when a pastor has lived through a traumatic experience. In the sermon "In His Time," which you read in the previous chapter, I mentioned my first battle with cancer, which involved me losing my voice for nine months. As you can imagine, that was a traumatic event since, as a pastor, I needed a voice to be able to preach. Because it was so traumatic and life-shaping, I have found myself mentioning that experience often. While my intention was not to call attention to myself but to illustrate the text, before long I came to believe that my cancer stories were a distraction.

The same thing happens to war veterans who end up back in the foxhole in almost every sermon. Of course, that traumatic experience relates to many sermons—especially those that have anything to do with faith or fear—but the overuse of the story renders the illustrations ineffective.

However, even if it is not the same story, too many personal stories are distracting. If you always talk about your golf game, people will start to wonder if you ever do anything besides play golf. If you are bald, you do not have to say something about it every week—we know, we can see. The same is true with your height, weight, or general appearance.

Besides, it is not always necessary to make the illustration personal. For instance, instead of saying, "I was watching the Super Bowl with some friends in 2008 when E-Trade's talking babies came on," why not just say, "Do you remember the iconic E-Trade talking babies ad from the 2008 Super Bowl?"

Suitable

Personal illustrations are powerful and, if used well, can help bring clarity and understanding to the text.[34] That is the bottom line:

---

34. "When used wisely and sparingly, personal stories clarify the text." Carter, Duvall, and Hays, *Preaching God's Word,* 135.

use them, but only use them if they are effective in illustrating the text. If they detract from the text, leave them out.[35]

About a decade ago, I heard a pastor use a personal illustration that involved his wife turning him down for sex that morning. This was too much information—even though he was teaching on marriage, it got in the way of the message.

Another time I was in the congregation of a pastor who returned to the pulpit after recuperating from surgery for several months. He showed a picture of his open wound from the surgery on the big screen. I am not especially squeamish, but I had to look away. In both instances, the inappropriate personal illustration is what I remember about the worship service. They capsized the sermon.

So how much is too much? Calvin Miller provides sage guidance: "How much should the story of your own pilgrimage hold its place among the various illustrations of the sermon? The answer gathers about the dividing line that separates narcissism from story force."[36]

Over the years, I have asked students to create guiding questions to ask themselves before using a personal illustration. Here's an edited version of their ideas:

- Is there a compelling reason to interject myself into the story?

- Would using this glorify God or me?

---

35. "If an illustration draws more attention to me than the text, it's off the table. People have a natural curiosity about the preacher's life. That's fine. However, to manipulate this for personal attention shows a deep insecurity; preachers willing to pander to that curiosity don't serve the text, they serve themselves." Smith, "Stage Lights."

36. Miller, *Preaching*, 164.

- Will telling this violate a trust?

- Will this diminish or enhance the message?

- Would it diminish the office of pastor for me to tell this story?

- Could this create an obstacle to others?

- Can I obtain the same result without making it personal?

- Have I talked about myself too much lately?

- Will this illustration assist in my goal of spiritual transformation?

- Does this have the potential to hurt someone or keep him or her from hearing my message?

- Will the congregation be able to relate to this story?

You might want to use my student's work as a starting point for creating your own pre-flight checklist. When used with care, personal illustrations can be powerful.

5

Fresh Illustrations

Shortly after I turned forty, our family moved from a congregation that was composed primarily of senior adults to a church near a military base that had mostly young families attending. Susan and I went from being one of the youngest couples of the church to one of the oldest. My sermons did not change that much, but my illustrations did. I had to freshen them up.

Personal, biblical, and hypothetical illustrations worked in both locations, but the preacher stories and canned illustrations that I was accustomed to using with the one church fell flat with the new congregation. In this case, it was not so much the surrounding culture but the church culture that made the difference. At the new church, the stories came across as bumpkin; they just didn't resonate with the people; they were not relevant.

At the time, there were no internet-based sermon illustration services (at least as far as I knew), due in large part to the internet's infancy. In the year 2000, churches were starting to get websites, but they certainly were not commonplace. If I was going to have fresh illustrations, I was going to have to write them.

Some of the change in my approach happened because of the demographic makeup of the new congregation. However, some of the transition from canned illustrations and preacher stories to fresh illustrations happened because of the era. Pastor John

Bisagno captures the mood at the time when he writes, "The story that illustrates the principle must always be relevant and fresh, something to which the hearer will instantly relate. Throw away those old illustration books and read *USA Today*, *Time*, *Newsweek*, *People*, and a major daily newspaper, and regularly view local and national newscasts."[1]

Three out of four of the effectiveness characteristics (see chapter 2) require congregational exegesis—an understanding of the people you are preaching to. Clarity does require some knowledge of the congregation, but for the most part, if the illustration is void of extraneous or erroneous details and has a connection to the text, it is green-lighted for clarity. However, the other three (familiarity, interest, and appropriateness) are heavily audience dependent.

To be effective,

- the subject matter must be familiar to the audience,

- the members of the congregation must find it interesting, and

- the listeners must feel it is appropriate.

Notice how these characteristics build on each other. Familiarity is foundational. If the people will not be familiar with the subject matter of the illustration, it will not be effective. Built upon familiarity is how interesting the illustration is. Will the people find the illustration's subject interesting? Does the illustration build interest in the text? After determining that the subject is both familiar and interesting, then preachers must determine if it is appropriate for the occasion.

---

1. Bisagno, *Principle Preaching*, 15.

Raiter writes, "The advantage of illustrations from newspapers and television is that you are then speaking of things with which people are familiar. Jesus' world of sheep and fishermen and fig trees is largely unfamiliar to most people."[2]

For an illustration to be effective, the subject matter needs to be in the congregation's consciousness; it needs to be readily accessible to them. In a multigenerational church, what is most accessible to the majority of the congregation is what is current, not an event from fifty years ago. While there will be a percentage of a West Coast congregation that will remember the Santa Barbara oil spill of 1969, many of the listeners would not have even been born. However, most will be aware of the 2018 wildfire that hit Paradise, California. The fresher the illustration is, the better it will likely work.[3]

This principle became even more vivid to me in January 2019. I have preached in ethnic and multicultural churches in the United States and have done some international speaking; however, I had never faced a challenge like I did when I did some teaching and preaching at a conference in the Philippines.

The teaching was a snap, largely due to the assistance of the local seminary faculty, who helped me contextualize my teaching during the question-and-answer sessions. The challenge was adapting the sermons written for middle-class California congregations to pastors serving in southeast Asia. I couldn't get help from the faculty after the fact during a Q&A time. I had to contextualize the sermons before preaching them.

---

2. Raiter, "On Sermons and Preaching," 97.

3. "An illustration that is true, has a point, and is believable still won't do any good if it doesn't grab and hold the listener's attention. That's why the newer the illustration, the better." Moyer, *Show Me How to Illustrate Evangelistic Sermons*, 23.

Of course, I did not change the sermon content—the teaching remained the same. But I did have to adapt the illustrations to the people's cultural context, which I knew little about before arriving in the country. Between sessions, I spent a good bit of time researching their culture on the internet, talking to locals, and rewriting sermon illustrations.

Even without the cross-cultural dynamic, contextualization is important. The Sermon Illustration Evaluation Rubric (chapter 2) considers the probable response from a specific congregation. The specific congregation matters. An illustration can be effective with one congregation and not another.

Since the ultimate test of effectiveness is with the specific congregation, it is safe to say that current illustrations—fresh illustrations—have a greater likelihood of being effective than illustrations that fell into our study's infrequently used cluster, like historical, fictional, or classic.

Again, this is congregationally dependent. If the congregation is primarily from a generation that shares a common knowledge of historical events, then historical illustrations will be familiar to them. If the congregation has a shared church culture, then classic illustrations might be more appropriate. But more times than not, the subject matter of fresh illustrations will be more familiar to an audience.[4] This is the primary strength of fresh illustrations. They are about people or subjects that are familiar to the people.

---

4. "Though some preachers are effective in the use of illustrations drawn from history, the arts, and literature, I am drawn to observations of human behavior and current events. In my view, the more people can identify with the illustration used, the more readily they can apply its point." Fuller, "Preaching and Education," 469.

Fresh Illustrations Are about Familiar People or Subjects

Familiar people. Because fresh illustrations tend to feature well-known people or current events, their subject matter is familiar to most people in the congregation. An example is the way Matthew Statler introduces his sermon "A Fruitful Farewell," based on Titus 3:8–15, with the following fresh illustration referring to the couple at the heart of the house remodeling and design show *Fixer Upper*:

> Chip and Joanna Gaines enter the house; outside, the roof is practically falling off, and inside, the floor is sagging. The people living inside are desperate. "Help us!" they scream internally. After some conversation and some vision casting, the scene goes to a commercial. We all wait in anticipation to see what happens to the house. Will it be renovated? Will the owners be happy with the changes? What unforeseen problems will arise? Reading Titus is like watching the first half of a renovation show. We don't get to see a full picture of the finished product. Will this congregation commit to good works? Will the truth of Jesus Christ's life, death, and resurrection transform these crumbling congregations into stately mansions?
>
> Probably everyone's favorite part of renovation shows is demolition day. Basically, everyone gets hammers and crowbars and gets to work stripping the house down to its bones. For this house to be structurally sound, the bones—the frame and foundations—have to be solid. What will be the fruit of their labor?
>
> Paul is concerned with faithful Christians. He tells Titus that these false teachers are causing problems, and it's wrecking the rest of the church. There are termites in the foundation. Time wasters have infiltrated the church.

Or worse, these false teachers are building a pagan temple, a temple to the god of self. Lest you think this doesn't apply to you, remember: every member of a local church is a brick in the structure; we all have a spot in this construction.[5]

After moving through the text verse by verse highlighting the need to address divisive ideas and people, then spending some time showing how people in the church need to be fruitful workers, Statler concludes the sermon by returning to the opening illustration:

When Chip and Joanna Gaines finish working on a house, they have this big canvas picture of what the house used to look like. The owners stand in front of this big picture and wait for Chip and Joanna to pull it apart and reveal what it looks like now. It is my prayer that when we get to the point in our lives where we pierce the veil from this life to the next, we will see clearly the fruits of our life. Will we be ashamed that we did not cultivate more fruit? Or will we be able to stand in front of our Lord and hear "Well done, good and faithful servant"? Our works do not save us; they only show that we are saved. [6]

Opening and closing the sermon with a renovation image from a popular television show draws attention to the work that needs to be done in the local church—there is constant renovation needed, not on the church building necessarily, but on the church itself. The introduction orients the listener to the work

---

5. Matthew Statler, "A Fruitful Farewell," https://sermons.faithlife.com/sermons/486931-a-fruitful-farewell.

6. Statler, "A Fruitful Farewell."

Paul writes about of addressing divisive ideas and divisive people. It draws attention to the text with an image that closely parallels what needs to be done in the church. Just as Chip Gaines demolishes the old to make way for the new, faithful people in the church need to uproot divisive ideas and discipline divisive people. The conclusion helps focus the attention of the congregation on the ultimate purpose of our work—to present the fruit of our labor before the Lord.

Statler could have used a personal illustration, if he had one, of a time when he did some home renovation, and it could have been equally effective, especially because of the power of a personal illustration to connect the preacher with the people. However, the same phenomenon happens with fresh illustrations. As Robinson says:

> Through illustrations, the preacher has revealed something about his reading, his thinking, and awareness of life. When some areas of a speaker's life overlap with the listeners', they are more likely to listen. He's gained some credibility. An ingredient in effective preaching is using specific material that connects with lives in the congregation.[7]

In essence, Statler's choice was one that helped connect him with his listeners. This would especially be true if they were fans of renovation shows in general or of the Gaines family in particular.

Statler also could have used a historical illustration by quoting from President Bush's speech to congress after the 9/11 terrorist attack on the Twin Towers, in which he said, "Tonight we welcome two leaders who embody the extraordinary spirit of all New Yorkers: Governor George Pataki and Mayor Rudolph Giuliani. As a symbol of America's resolve, my administration will work

---

7. Robinson, *Making a Difference in Preaching*, 32.

with Congress, and these two leaders, to show the world that we will rebuild New York City."[8]

But his fresh illustration was likely the right choice because it would likely appeal to more people. A few years ago, Susan and I attended a convention in Dallas, Texas and made two side trips. Before the meeting, we went to the George W. Bush Presidential Library housed on the SMU campus. After the meeting, we drove two hours to Waco so we could visit Joanna Gaines's Magnolia Market at the Silos.

The contrast was stark. I could not believe the number of people and the level of buzz that surrounded the Silos, compared with the few visitors we encountered at the presidential library. So, Statler could have used a historical illustration from President Bush's speech, and it would have paralleled this sermon's renovation concept, but I suspect that people in Statler's congregation found that his choice to introduce and conclude his sermon with a fresh illustration was a good one. It helped the people understand and apply Paul's point in Titus 3 and likely appealed to more members of the congregation than the historical alternative would have.

Familiar challenges. Not all fresh illustrations need to be about recognizable people like Chip and Joanna Gaines. Sometimes they can be about relatively unknown people who encounter a familiar challenge—like forgiving someone who harmed you. Here's one about a mother who lived out Matthew 6:14–15 in extreme circumstances:

> A mother's decision to forgive the boy who murdered her only son has had a bigger impact than she could have

---

8. Bush, "Address to a Joint Session of Congress on Thursday Night, September 20, 2001."

imagined. In 1993, a 16-year-old killed Mary Johnson's son Laramiun during an argument at a party. Mary wanted justice and said the killer, Oshea Israel, deserved to be caged because he was an animal. A jury convicted Israel of the crime and sentenced him to 25 and a half years in prison. A few years later, Mary asked authorities if she could visit Israel in prison. During that visit, Mary forgave her son's killer and began a new relationship with him.

When authorities released Israel from prison years later, Mary introduced him to her property owner and helped him get an apartment in the building where she lived. She said she has been able to forgive Israel because the Lord has helped her. She says originally her motives were selfish, but her perspective has changed. Mary said, "Unforgiveness is like cancer. It will eat you from the inside out. The forgiveness is for me. It's for me." Israel said he hasn't completely forgiven himself, but he is learning. He is working at a recycling plant during the day and is attending college at night. He wants to pay back Mary's forgiveness by contributing to society. Speaking to a group about his experience, Israel said, "A conversation can take you a long way."[9]

This is a remarkable story about forgiving in extreme circumstances. The unusual circumstances are what make this illustration so powerful. If Johnson could forgive her son's murderer, then we should be able to forgive people who commit lesser offenses against us. The illustration underscores that it is only possible

---

9. Jim L. Wilson, "Mother Chooses to Forgive Her Son's Murderer," https://sermons.faithlife.com/sermons/118886-mother-chooses-to-forgive-her -son's-murderer.

through God's power. The circumstances are unusual, but the struggle to forgive is very familiar to most people.

Another example of a familiar challenge is controlling the tongue:

> In *Today's Christian Woman*, Ramona Cramer Tucker writes about a moment in time that her friend Michelle wishes she could relive. After a business lunch in a restaurant, Michelle and Sharon went to the ladies' room. While they were fixing their makeup, their small talk took a sinister turn into gossip. Michelle and Sharon began lambasting a coworker who drove them both crazy. For a full two minutes, Michelle criticized her. The quiet that followed was interrupted by the familiar sound of a bathroom stall door opening. Glancing into the mirror, they watched in horror as an embarrassed, angry, red-faced coworker walked out. According to Tucker, "Michelle and Beth stared at each other in embarrassed panic. Michelle knew she couldn't take her words back. In the instant their eyes met, Beth fled out the door."
>
> Michelle never saw Beth again. Beth never came back to work. She resigned. Tucker writes, "While other staff members cheered what seemed to be good news, Michelle felt miserable. She wished she had talked to Beth instead of talking about Beth."[10]

The constant battle many have with worry is a third familiar challenge. Pastors Ernie Arnold and Nathan Pellegra both use medical information about worrying to illustrate Philippians 4:6–7. Arnold quotes a medical doctor to demonstrate the negative

---

10. Jim L. Wilson, "Is It Really 'Only Words'? (Prov. 16:28)," https://sermons.faithlife.com/sermons/79934-is-it-really-%22only-words%22.

effects of worry before making a pithy, memorable comment about the senselessness of worry:

> Dr. Charles Mayo states that "worry affects the circulation, the heart, the glands, the entire nervous system." He also states that he never knew of a person who had died from overworking, but he did know of many who died due to worry. A person can worry themselves into bad health and even death. But you will never worry yourself into a longer life.[11]

Pellegra takes a similar tack. He shows, from a medical point of view, that worry creates physical, mental, and social problems.

> I am reminded of an article that I read from the Communications Doctor that said, "Eighty-five percent of what we worry about never comes true," but unfortunately, the good doctor's prescriptions did not amount to more than systematically writing down and categorizing our worries. If that is all the medicine we have for worry, we are in deep trouble. The physical effects that worry has on the human body are staggering. The same article states,

>> "Chemicals released during extended periods of worry wreak havoc on our physical being, with symptoms ranging from headaches to high blood pressure. Chronic worriers are prone to heart conditions and as a general rule are not too much fun to be around. Thus worriers often experience feelings of loneliness

---

11. Ernie L. Arnold, "Stress/Worry/Anxiety and the Christian Life," https://sermons.faithlife.com/sermons/126191-stressworryanxiety-and-the-christian-life.

and isolation as individuals flee from their forecasts
of doom and gloom."[12]

In these cases, the preachers use fresh illustrations to demonstrate an intersection of life and the Bible. It is not that they made the biblical teaching credible or relevant. The Bible is credible. It is relevant. We don't need illustrations to make it so. However, illustrations can reveal the Bible's credibility and relevance as preachers show how its teachings work in normal life. Old Testament professor David Deuel writes, "Avoid being oblique, obscure, pedantic, or using outdated illustrations to which people cannot relate. Show how the timeless truths of the word of God touch their everyday lives."[13]

This is the secondary function for fresh illustrations. They showcase an intersection between the Bible and the contemporary world. A steady diet of fresh illustrations can help audience members better appreciate the Bible's relevance to life's challenges.

Fresh Illustrations Are Based on Subjects That Many Will Find Interesting

Fresh illustrations grab the listeners' attention. In part, this is because their subject matter is familiar, but beyond that threshold, the reason it is familiar is because a publisher, filmmaker, or reporter found it interesting. Catholic priest Richard Hart makes this point, writing, "Listeners will be more attentive if we use items from the news. If it is timely or current and fits the subject matter, it enables the preacher to illustrate some idea in a forceful way."[14]

---

12.   Nathan Pellegra, "Philippians 4:4–9," https://sermons.faithlife.com/sermons/64275-philippians-4-4-9.

13.   Deuel, "Expository Preaching from Old Testament Narrative," 300.

14.   Hart, "Illustrations Enliven Our Preaching," 22.

In his sermon "The Path to Greatness," Rusty Russell weaves several news items into a sermon illustration that shows the amount of narcissism in pop culture.

> Ever heard of NPD? Probably not. It stands for "narcissistic personality disorder." That's right! There's actually a psychological condition describing many Americans' fascination with themselves. By the way, it's a problem that isn't just growing; it's exploding! According to Jean Twenge, the psychologist who wrote *The Narcissism Epidemic*, one out of every ten Americans in their twenties has suffered some symptoms of NPD.

Russell gives some examples of the narcissistic behavior epidemic, including a girl on reality TV who wants a marching band for her sixteenth birthday party, fake paparazzi you can hire for yourself, and self-branding. He then continues:

> Although these seem like a random collection of current trends, all are rooted in a single underlying shift in the American psychology: the relentless rise of narcissism in our culture. Not only are there more narcissists than ever, but non-narcissistic people are seduced by the increasing emphasis on material wealth, physical appearance, celebrity worship, and attention seeking. Standards have shifted, sucking otherwise humble people into the vortex of granite countertops, tricked-out social media pages, and plastic surgery. A popular dance track repeats the words "money, success, fame, glamour" over and over, declaring that all other values have "either been discredited or destroyed."[15]

---

15. Rusty Russell, "The Path to Greatness: Suffering," https://sermons. faithlife.com/sermons/112724-the-path-to-greatness:-suffering.

The "stacking" of observations about pop culture helps draw his audience's attention to the problem, preparing them to hear the solution he offers in his sermon.

Strange happenings. York and Decker encourage using examples of strange happenings to form the basis of interesting fresh illustrations. They write, "We also recommend quirkier sources. Learn to look for illustrations where no one else is looking. We particularly like books about strange and unusual oddities and peculiarities of history or culture."[16]

Francis Chan does that in his book *Crazy Love: Overwhelmed by a Relentless God*:

> Stan [Gerlach] was giving a eulogy at a memorial service when he decided to share the gospel. At the end of his message, Stan told the mourners, "You never know when God is going to take your life. At that moment, there's nothing you can do about it. Are you ready?" Then Stan sat down, fell over, and died. His wife and sons tried to resuscitate him, but there was nothing they could do—just as Stan had said a few minutes earlier.[17]

It is ironic that the preacher would mention that a person can die at any moment right before he dies. But it certainly illustrates James 4:13–14, doesn't it?

Other examples of how unusual illustrations can drive home a point well are the following stories about a priceless automobile that was once valued at only a dollar and the painting that increased in value after it was shredded.

---

16. York and Decker, *Preaching with Bold Assurance,* 169.

17. Jim L. Wilson, "Man Dies Moments after Delivering Eulogy," https://sermons.faithlife.com/sermons/111494-man-dies-moments-after-delivering-eulogy.

Concept Car Sold for a Dollar Transformed to $4.2 Million Worth Illustrates 1 Corinthians 7:23

In the early 1960s, the Lincoln Futura concept car created for a 1955 auto show was not worth much. It was used in a 1959 movie and then sold to automobile designer George Barris for one dollar. Since it was untitled and could not be insured, the car had little value and was relegated to a back parking lot. In January 2013, the same car sold for over four million dollars at an auto auction. What made the difference?

In 1965, Barris used the forgotten concept car as the basis for the 19-foot-long Batmobile from the 1960s television series *Batman*. Facing a deadline from producers to come up with a design for a crime-fighting vehicle for Batman and Robin, Barris took the Futura from the back of his building and went to work. The car became known as "Batmobile number one" because it was the first one used on the program, although several copies were built later. At the auction, hopeful owners pushed the price higher than most expected it would go. The auction company revealed the selling price but did not disclose the name of the winning bidder. A spokesman for George Barris says the designer was pleased with the auction results.

In this case, the car's value increased because Batman drove it in a TV show, not because of its general usefulness. Christians' value is determined not by what they do for God but by the fact that they belong to him, and he was willing to pay the ultimate price for them.[18]

---

18. Jim L. Wilson and Jim Sandell, "Concept Car Sold for a Dollar Transforms to $4.2 Million Worth," https://sermons.faithlife.com/sermons/122220-concept-car-sold-for-a-dollar-transforms-to-dollar4.2-million-worth.

Painting Worth More after It Was Destroyed
Illustrates Psalm 51:16–17's Teaching
about the Value of Brokenness

The anonymous buyer had no idea that Banksy had built a shredder into the frame of his 2006 painting, *Girl with a Balloon* when she paid $1.37 million for it. Instead of attempting to nullify the purchase with Sotheby's, she decided to hold on to the "piece of art history." In an ironic twist, the half-shredded painting increased in value after it was partially destroyed.

Most of the time, broken things are worthless; however, there are some things that are worth even more after they are broken.[19]

Both illustrations stimulate interest in the concept of value because of the irony inherent in how they increased in value. The irony grabs people's attention, readying them to hear the biblical point.

As with other types of illustrations, the congregation's familiarity and interest in the subject matter of a fresh illustration does not mean it should be used. Even if it is clear—well written, without needless details—and closely parallels the text, it still should not be used unless it is appropriate.

How can you tell if a fresh illustration is appropriate? Bob Vacendak builds tension and creates interest with the following illustration from his sermon "Responding to a Clear and Present Danger":

---

19. Jim L. Wilson, "Painting Worth More after It Was Destroyed," https://sermons.faithlife.com/sermons/321483-painting-worth-more-after-it-was-destroyed.

In an interview on the TV show *Inside Edition*, Anne Hjelle [yell-aye] shared the following words about her horrible ordeal: "Once he started clamping down, I remember thinking, 'This is it. I'm going to die.' "

Riding her mountain bike in a Southern California wilderness park, Anne was ferociously attacked by a mountain lion. Thrown off her bike, Anne immediately knew what was happening. She said the lion "was going for my neck, and his goal, as it would be with any type of prey, was to break my neck and paralyze me."

Fortunately, Anne's friend Debbie Nichols, who had been riding with her, came to the rescue. Seeing Anne being dragged into the brush, Debbie began a tug of war with the lion. Debbie pulled on Anne's legs while the lion held Anne's face and head in his jaws. Two other bikers came by and tried to scare the animal away. Finally, the lion let go, backing off his prey.

Anne was airlifted to a hospital. Rangers hunting the lion found the partially eaten body of Mike Reynolds, another biker. The animal had made the kill before attacking Anne. The Rangers found the lion hovering near the body and killed it.

Face scarred, facing reconstructive surgery, Anne tells what went on inside her in that terrifying ordeal as she grappled with the lion for her life: "I was terrified. My first words, as soon as he grabbed on to me, were 'Jesus help me.' It was a conscious decision; I'm in serious trouble and I need help."[20]

---

20. Bob Vacendak, "Responding to a Clear and Present Danger," https://sermons.faithlife.com/sermons/258132-sunday-april-15-2018.

I would green-light this illustration for familiarity—most would relate to going for a bike ride. I would also green-light it for clarity. He does a good job of writing a clear illustration. Interesting? Of course, it is interesting. This illustration is literally about life and death. However, I'd yellow-light it for appropriateness, and if I knew that there were a lot of children in the room, I'd red-light it because of the mature subject matter and the vivid description—mangled face, partially eaten body; those images could cause nightmares for younger people in the crowd.

However, that is not to say that preachers cannot use illustrations that involve death. In my sermon "Off with the Old, On with the New," based on Hebrews 10:16–17, I tell the following story to illustrate sacrificing one's life for another:

> While on vacation in Florida, Gareth Griffith decided to try skydiving. He was jumping in tandem with Michael Costello, an experienced instructor.
>
> Something went wrong.
>
> The main chute failed to open. No big deal; they had a backup chute. The backup failed too. The two men went into a violent spin as they plummeted to their destiny. The instructor corrected the spin and regained control of the fall. Griffith was on bottom, and the instructor was on top.
>
> As they neared the ground, the instructor folded his arms and legs, causing the pair to rotate. Because of this move, the instructor hit the ground first, cushioning his student's blow.
>
> Griffith survived. Costello wasn't so lucky—he sacrificed his own life so that Griffith could live.
>
> Jesus sacrificed his life for us, but it wasn't just to show his love for us; it was to provide a way of escape—it was so we could live. The new covenant is our only chance. If we sin by rejecting Christ's sacrifice for our sins, we have

no hope. Verses 26 and 27 say, "For if we deliberately go on sinning after receiving the knowledge of the truth, there no longer remains a sacrifice for sins, but a terrifying expectation of judgment and the fury of a fire about to consume the adversaries."

Christ's sacrifice was so we could experience eternal life, which is not a reward for living well but the result of the effectual working of Christ's death on the cross. Grace is the only provision for our salvation. [21]

I preached this sermon in a church that had all the younger children in a separate service. I did not fear that the illustration would disturb the audience. Also, the illustration does not use death gratuitously—the sacrificial death of the skydiving instructor does not fully capture what Jesus did for us on the cross—but it does parallel the willingness of one person to die so that another can live.

Fresh illustrations based on movies. Sermon illustrations from movies can be tricky. One of the difficulties of using movie-based illustrations is that there could be an implied endorsement. [22] This is especially problematic if the illustration is from an R-rated movie. [23]

---

21. Jim L. Wilson, "Off with the Old, On with the New (Hebrews 10:16–27)," https://sermons.faithlife.com/sermons/79978-off-with-the-old-on-with-the-new.

22. "Suppose I want to illustrate from a movie. When I stand up as a pastor in a worship service and I name a movie, it comes across as an implied endorsement of that movie. I may want to use only one scene, which is morally impeccable; but I can't assume my hearers are going to hear it that way. They'll hear, Oh, he went to that movie. He must have liked it because he's talking about it." Miller, "3 Questions to Ask When Preaching from Pop Culture."

23. "Using contemporary movies or television for illustrations demands sensitivity to the conscience of others. As a general rule, don't refer to movies or television shows that you cannot recommend. Stay away from references

However, fresh illustrations based on movies can also be very effective. This one from the movie *Finding Nemo* illustrates the teaching of Proverbs 3:12 that a father will discipline a son that he loves:

> In the Disney/Pixar animated feature *Finding Nemo*, Nemo is a little clownfish who is in big trouble. In an act of rebellion against his father, Nemo defiantly swims away from the safety of the oceanic reef where he lives to touch a boat anchored in the open ocean. Before he can return to safety, Nemo is captured by a diver and whisked away in a plastic container.
>
> He finds himself captive in a tank in a dentist's office in Sydney, Australia. He makes friends with the other fish in the tank, but each of them knows the hopelessness of their situation. Nemo is nearly killed when an angelfish named Gill convinces him to try to help everyone escape to the open ocean. After the failed escape attempt, Nemo is dejected. He knows that certain death is ahead, and there is nothing he can do about it. Even Gill, who was so enthusiastic about the possibility of escape, has lost all hope of ever leaving the tank that traps them. Nemo is not aware that his dedicated father has been fighting the odds to find and rescue him. Just when hope seems lost, Nemo's strength is renewed when he learns his father cares and is on the way to save him.

OPTION I: Play clip from *Finding Nemo*, Chapter 17, News Travels, 58:50 to 1:00:37, and make application.

---

to R-rated movies or other forms of offensive entertainment, even if you did not personally see them." York and Decker, *Preaching with Bold Assurance*, 170.

OPTION II: Describe scene as follows and make application.

The news of Nemo's impending rescue comes from Nigel, a pelican who lives in Sydney Harbour. To get to Nemo, Nigel runs into the window and hides when the dentist comes to open it. Afterward, Nigel keeps a wary eye out for the dentist and whispers toward the fish tank, "Hey, Hey, Psssst!" One of the fish in the tank who knows Nigel says, "Hey Nigel. You just missed an extraction." Momentarily distracted, Nigel asks, "Oh, has he loosened the periodontal ligament with the elevator yet?" Then, remembering why he came, Nigel says, "What am I talking about? Nemo. Where's Nemo? I've got to speak with him."

Hearing his name, Nemo swims up. "What, what is it?" Nigel points at the clownfish and begins his explanation. "Your dad's been fighting the entire ocean looking for you!" Nemo acts confused, but perks up: "My father? Really?" Nigel continues the story. "He's traveled hundreds of miles. He has been battling sharks, jellyfish, and all sorts of …"

Nemo interrupts, "Sharks?" He shakes his head, "That can't be him." Nigel looks at Nemo and asks, "Are you sure?" Searching his memory, he begins, "What was his name? Some sort of sport fish or something. Tuna? Trout?" Nemo injects, "Marlin?" Nigel practically shouts, "That's it! Marlin, the little clownfish from the reef." Hearing this news, Nemo starts to get excited. Speaking to the fish around him, he says, "It's my dad. He took on a shark!" Nigel holds up three feathered fingers. "I heard he took on three." The other fish respond, "Three?" One of them quickly does the math adding, "That's gotta be 4,800 teeth!"

Nigel continues the story. "You see kid, after you were taken by diver Dan over there, your dad followed the boat you were on like a maniac." Nemo's attention is fully focused on Nigel as he asks, "Really?" The music begins to swell as Nigel tells and acts out the story. "He's swimming and swimming. He's giving it all he's got. Three gigantic sharks capture him, and he blows them up. Then he dives thousands of feet, where he gets chased by a monster with huge teeth. He ties this thing to the rock. What does he get for a reward? He gets to battle an entire jellyfish forest." Nearly out of breath, Nigel slows down. "By now, he's riding on a bunch of sea turtles on the East Australian Current. The word is, he's heading this way right now to Sydney." The fish all cheer, but Nemo is no longer with them. Knowing his father cares and is coming for him renews Nemo's hope. He has to follow through on the escape plan and be successful this time. When he completes the task, Gill encourages Nemo again saying, "That took guts, kid."

APPLICATION: Fathers have great responsibility for their families. Most children will never know the extent of the sacrifices their fathers make for them or what they are willing to do to protect them. Marlin wasn't trying to ruin Nemo's fun when he warned him against swimming away from the oceanic reef; he was trying to protect Nemo. Nemo confused caution with a lack of courage. In the end, Nemo came to understand that having one doesn't mean you don't have the other. [24]

---

24. Jim L. Wilson and Jim Sandell, "'Finding Nemo' Movie: Dad Was Just Trying to Protect His Son," https://sermons.faithlife.com/sermons/98739-%22finding-nemo%22-movie:-dad-was-just-trying-to-protect-his-son.

Should you show a clip or tell the story? Notice that this illustration is long and would take a significant amount of time to tell, far longer than the two minutes it would take to show the clip. However, before you ask your sound tech to hit the play button, there are several things to think about.

- Public showing of movie clips requires a license to comply with copyright laws.[25]

- Technology often has technical difficulties. Whether it is user error or mechanical breakdown, a prolonged pause to address technology issues is a sermon killer.

- Because visual media is so powerful, it can take attention away from the point—it can be interesting but not create interest in the text.

- Some research suggests that showing video clips can hinder, not enhance, imagination.

In his article "Sanctuary as Cinema?: Screens Should Not Block the Story," Pastor Kevin Bergeson writes:

We have found that sometimes using movie clips can limit people's own imaginations. Ask anyone who voraciously read all *The Hunger Games* trilogy and who then saw the first movie how the book and movie compared. Did it work seamlessly for them? Similarly, what if someone had an image in their mind of the Sea of Galilee and how Jesus calmed the waves and wind and then was presented with a video of the Galilee that was taken only a few weeks

---

25. See https://us.cvli.com/ for details on getting a license for showing movie clips in your church.

ago? Is this a biblical scene or not? After seeing this new image, peoples' imaginations are no longer shaped by the story itself and how it has worked in their own lives of faith but by the reality of the present contours of this lake. How do we balance the power of imagination and the power of movies? Don't let the clip smother the work of the Holy Spirit firing the imaginations of the listeners. Let the text speak![26]

Just as a spoken illustration can shine a light on the text or blind a person from seeing the truth of the text, a visual can either enhance or hinder imagination. It can open minds or close doors.

For most preachers, fresh illustrations will take more time to write than the other types in the frequently used cluster because they require more research. Preachers can develop personal or biblical illustrations quickly because of their familiarity with their own experiences and Bible stories. Often, preachers insert them into a sermon extemporaneously when they perceive that a congregation needs additional clarification. The same is true with hypothetical illustrations. Though they may prepare them ahead of time, preachers often create hypothetical illustrations as they are preaching.

With fresh illustrations, preachers will need to spend time reading websites, magazines, and books. Not that all of this would be specifically research; if they go to movies, watch TV, or attend sporting events, they will encounter items from pop culture that can become sermon illustration material. However, even when an event comes to mind from previous exposure, preachers will still need to research the material to make sure they are factual and accurate when they develop the illustration.

---

26. Bergeson, "Sanctuary as Cinema," 303.

Rarely do fresh illustrations happen quickly. Even if preachers do not write original fresh illustrations, they still have to find them from sermon illustration sources, which takes time. However, it is time well spent.

Fresh illustrations are an effective way to shine light on the biblical text. Their subject matter, by definition, is familiar and interesting. If preachers find a story that closely parallels the biblical situation and are careful to leave out extraneous details, they can be green-lighted for clarity. The greatest challenge in using fresh illustrations is to make sure they do not overpower the text and are appropriate for the occasion.

6

Biblical Illustrations

In their sermons, some preachers obtain a balance among the various genres of the Bible. Others have an imbalanced approach, gravitating toward a particular genre and occasionally preaching a sermon outside of their preference. However, they tend to achieve some balance by using the other genres as supporting material. For instance, preachers who tend to base their sermons on biblical narratives often quote from the Epistles to reinforce their sermon's point. Those who prefer the Epistles tend to use the biblical narratives as illustration material to help their congregation understand, apply, or experience the New Testament teaching.[1]

For preachers who primarily preach from the Epistles, using biblical illustrations has an obvious upside: their congregations are getting greater exposure to the full counsel of God than if they did not use such illustrations. The illustration fulfills its primary function of assisting members of the congregation understand, apply,

---

1. "The Old Testament can also be utilized in our preaching by making use of examples or illustrations of New Testament truths. Negative examples of sinfulness abound in the Old Testament, and these reinforce and visualize our understanding of the New Testament's teaching of our utter depravity before a holy God." Hamilton, *Preaching with Balance*, 109.

or experience the text.[2] But it also fulfills a secondary function of exposing the congregation to a broad spectrum of biblical material.

Most illustration types expose the listeners to extrabiblical information. As mentioned in chapter 4, one of the strengths of personal illustrations is that they reveal the preacher's life to the listeners, increasing the connection between preacher and congregation. Fresh illustrations provide information about the intersection of culture and faith (chapter 5), and historical illustrations increase historical literacy (chapter 8). Biblical illustrations expose congregation members not to extrabiblical material but to additional biblical material. One of the strengths of biblical illustrations is how they keep the focus on God's word even while providing examples that help the congregation members understand, apply, or experience the text. As pastor Nelson Price writes, "Biblical illustrations are superior to most and tend to stir the listener's overall interest in Scripture."[3]

Another distinction between other types of illustrations and biblical illustrations is that they, unlike other types of illustrations, are authoritative.[4] Thus, preachers must handle biblical illustrations differently. If it is ever appropriate to shape an illustration

---

2. "Text-driven application must include practical illustrations, examples, and suggestions so that the audience can adopt and model their lives after the biblical truth being taught. The best place to begin, in my judgment, is with biblical examples. The Old Testament in particular contains a reservoir of resources. One should then proceed to the here and now, taking into careful consideration the specific context in which one ministers the word." Akin, "Applying a Text-Driven Sermon," 273.

3. Price, "Preaching and Church Growth," 489.

4. "Using Scripture to illustrate and support the points of a sermon also strengthens the authority of a message." Thomas, "Bible Translations and Expository Preaching," 327.

to fit a sermon, it is definitely not appropriate when using biblical illustrations.

Should Preachers Use Biblical Illustrations?

There is not a consensus among preachers and homileticians about whether preachers should use biblical illustrations. The lack of consensus about this or any other issue is not surprising; experts and practitioners tend to have various viewpoints. What is noteworthy is the intensity of their opinions. Most of those in favor of using biblical illustrations have strong convictions about using them, often arguing for their exclusive use. Those who warn against their use are adamant that biblical illustrations should be avoided.

Champions of biblical illustrations. John MacArthur champions the use of biblical illustrations for four reasons: "Because they teach the Word while they illustrate, because they are God's choice of illustrative material, because Scripture interprets itself best, and because they have divine authority to go with human interest."[5]

MacArthur uses biblical illustrations because of their secondary function of exposing the congregation to additional biblical material, but there is more to his argument than that distinction. He says they are "God's choice of illustrative material," likely a reference to the New Testament writers' use of Old Testament narratives. MacArthur also notes that they have authority that other illustration types lack and that they fulfill another function: they interpret the text. No other illustration type is authoritative or able to interpret the text—only biblical illustrations do that.

---

5. MacArthur, "Rightly Dividing the Word of Truth," 88.

David Deuel does not use biblical illustrations exclusively but prefers them because of their authority and ability to instruct, not just explain. He writes:

> I look primarily for biblical illustrations. The New Testament writers used the Old Testament for illustrations more than any other source. It is appropriate to use illustrations from other sources, but I prefer biblical ones for two reasons. Biblical illustrations, unlike nonbiblical ones, have authority. Illustrations from other sources may be interesting and help hearers grasp a point better, but they are not the inspired Word of God. A second reason I prefer biblical illustrations is that they teach, as well as illustrate. They expand your people's knowledge of the Bible.[6]

Those who champion biblical illustrations do so, in large part, because of the source. They see an advantage to the illustration being from the inspired word of God. In an ironic twist, the authoritative nature of the source material is also the reason that some dissenting voices warn against their use.

Dissenting voices. Pastor Jay Adams warns against using biblical material as sermon illustrations for the very reason those who champion its use cite for using biblical illustrations almost exclusively: their authoritative nature. He puts it this way:

> Many preachers use Scripture, especially the Old Testament, illustratively. Don't do it. Always use the Bible authoritatively; never illustratively. Scripture was not given merely to illustrate points; it was written to make points. If you don't pay attention to this warning, the first thing

---

6. Deuel, "Expository Preaching from Old Testament Narrative," 294.

you know, you will find yourself making points you want to make and using (misusing) the Bible to illustrate and back up your ideas. Psychologizers do this all the time.[7]

Pastor and professor Donald Sunukjian joins Adams in this dissent. In a chapter addressing "dubious supporting or amplifying materials" that should be avoided, he includes a section on biblical illustrations alongside sections on dictionary definitions, statistics, quotations, and parallel passages. He begins the section by writing, "The time to teach a biblical story is when it is the primary passage for your message, not when it is a secondary illustration of another passage. In other words, you should preach the story of Joseph and his brothers as a part of a series through Genesis and not as an illustration of Romans 8:28 (i.e., that all things work together for good)."[8]

Sunukjian objects to illustrating Romans 8:28 with Genesis 50:20 because "the point of Genesis 50:20 is that God used the brothers' evil intentions to bring about good circumstances in Joseph's life. But that is not the point of Romans 8:28. The point of Romans 8:28–30 is that God will work in your sufferings and weaknesses to produce the good character of Christlikeness."[9]

While Sunukjian states that he objects to using the Genesis 50 narrative as a sermon illustration for Romans 8:28, he does not mention if he objects to alluding to Romans 8:28 when preaching a narrative sermon on Genesis 50. If one is appropriate, is the other?

In his sermon "Therefore Part Seven: All Things Work Together," Russell Jeffares uses Joseph's encounter with his

---

7. Adams, *Preaching with Purpose*, 103.

8. Sunukjian, *Invitation to Biblical Preaching*, 133.

9. Sunukjian, *Invitation to Biblical Preaching*, 133.

brothers in Genesis 50:20 to illustrate Romans 8:28.[10] On the other hand, Paul Hawkins cites Romans 8:28 as a cross-reference when preaching Joseph's story with a narrative structure in his sermon "Joseph in Prison."[11] In my view, both these preachers appropriately allowed Scripture to interpret Scripture when they connected the verses to one another.

While I agree with Sunukjian's observation that the point of the narrative used as an illustration needs to match the point of the primary text, I do not see a contradiction in this particular case, primarily because I see the point of Genesis 50:20 as having less to do with good circumstances for Joseph and more to do with God's redemptive purpose. Through Joseph's brothers' evil actions, God put Joseph into a strategic position to be able to provide for God's chosen people during the famine. I bring this up not to quibble with Sunukjian but rather to point out that people tend to view things differently.

In addition, in the quote cited above, he does not include verses 29–30—he only mentions Romans 8:28. This raises another hermeneutical challenge. Context is king. Taken by itself, Romans 8:28 does fit Joseph's statement to his brothers in Genesis 50:20, but placed in context with the other two verses, the point develops a sharper focus. Nevertheless, even with the expansion, producing character is part of God's redemptive purpose. While there is not a direct statement in the Genesis narrative, it is implied that God used Joseph's trials, brought about by the brothers' evil act, to develop character in him.

---

10. Russell Jeffares, "Therefore Part Seven: All Things Work Together," https://sermons.faithlife.com/sermons/281053-therefore-part-seven-all-things-work-together.

11. Paul Hawkins, "Joseph in Prison," https://sermons.faithlife.com/sermons/26311-joseph-in-prison.

When Joseph was wearing the garment of favoritism, he presented himself as a brash, immature, entitled young man. However, when we encounter him in Genesis 50, while wearing the garment of exultation, he is a humble man focused on serving others. It is not a leap to say that God used the trials in Joseph's life to produce character in him, which is an observation I feel comfortable cross-referencing with Romans 5:3–5.

This particular case aside, Sunukjian makes three further arguments against using biblical illustrations:

- The customs and culture of biblical times are so foreign that the modern audience will not relate to them.

- Preachers often use a biblical story to illustrate a point, even when the point of the story and the point of the passage being illustrated are not the same.

- A biblical story may simply repeat a point, not apply it.[12]

Pastor and professor Vern Charette counters the dissent of Adams and Sunukjian with an observation that the New Testament writers used Old Testament stories as illustrations.[13] I'm not as quick to dismiss Adams's and Sunukjian's arguments. It's not that I agree that biblical illustrations are off limits, but these authors' observations are valid and should be addressed

---

12. Sunukjian, *Invitation to Biblical Preaching*, chapter 6.

13. "Though men like Adams and Sunukjian say not to use the Old Testament for illustrations, a look at the New Testament's usage of the Old indeed reveals that the biblical authors used the Old Testament for illustrations." Charette, "Keeping Your People Glued," 48.

when crafting illustrations and deciding whether to use them. In short, we need to use biblical illustrations well.

Using Biblical Illustrations Well

In my sermon "God Is Faithful, Even When We Are Not," from Lamentations 3:22–24, I could have used a personal illustration about God's faithfulness, but I chose instead to use a pair of biblical illustrations—one from a narrative passage, the other from a parable. God certainly has been faithful to me, and to the congregation to whom I was preaching, but I thought the biblical stories would better help the people experience God's faithfulness. Here's how I closed the sermon:

> Let me close out our message today by telling you two stories, one from the Old Testament, the other from the New.
>
> I'm not sure how the word got to Hosea. Perhaps he overheard a whisper as he walked by the townspeople, or maybe it was as a result of a tireless search. But Hosea heard that there was going to be an auction—a prostitute auction—and he heard Gomer was up for sale.
>
> He gathered what little resources he had and went to the auction.
>
> Naked, Gomer stood before the crowd that gathered to bid on prostitutes as a farmer would bid on a pig. "How much do I hear for this one?" the auctioneer said. Amid the snide comments and lewd remarks, the local prophet, Hosea, spoke up. "I'll give you fifteen pieces of silver." The crowd quieted. "Is that his wife?" someone whispered. "Is she the one that married the prophet?"
>
> "Yes, I've got fifteen pieces of silver, and a homer and a half of barley." What had he done? He'd bid everything he

had. Shouldn't he have started low and moved up? What if someone outbid him? He'd be humiliated.

"I've got a bid for fifteen pieces of silver and a homer and a half of barley. Do I hear any more?" The auctioneer asked. "Going once. Going twice. Sold! To the man with the silver and the barley."

Hosea made his way through the crowd, paid the price, and walked toward Gomer. He placed his robe around his bride and said, "Come on, Gomer, we're going home."

Finally, after hitting rock bottom, the son "came to his senses." He did just as he said he would. He got up out of the "slimy pit" and took the first step toward home. One step followed another until he could see the old homestead.

But before he could see his father, his father saw him and began to run to him. The dad threw his arms around the son and kissed him. The boy began his speech: "I have sinned against heaven and in your sight; I am no longer worthy to be called your son." But before he could finish, the father interrupted and called for his servants. "Look at my son—he doesn't have proper clothes. Get him a robe, and some sandals, and put a family ring on his finger! My dead son is now alive! Let's celebrate! Finally, he's home."

God is faithful, even when we're not. He's the prophet that buys back the prostitute wife; he's the father that welcomes home the prodigal son. He's faithful, even when we're not.[14]

---

14. Jim L. Wilson, "God Is Faithful, Even When We Are Not," https://sermons.faithlife.com/sermons/79921-god-is-faithful-even-when-we-are-not.

The preachers in our study group used enough biblical illustrations to put it in the frequently used cluster. I agree with them that preachers should use biblical illustrations often, primarily for the reasons their proponents cite. However, when we use them, we should use them responsibly after weighing their potential for effectiveness, like any other type of sermon illustration (chapter 2), and remember that we are handling the word of truth when we summarize the stories.

Here's something I did not do well in the first of the two illustrations above. In retrospect, I wish I would not have imposed my idea of what an auction is like today onto the transaction Hosea made when he purchased Gomer. My point of reference was the farm auctions I attended as a child growing up in West Texas, and I imposed that experience on the text. In the illustration, I spoke of "snide comments and lewd remarks," while the text does not indicate that either took place. Heeding Adams's and Sunukjian's warnings, I wish I had taken greater care in my handling of the biblical narrative and stuck to what the text said happened, augmented by research into the customs of the day.

Though preachers will need to evaluate each specific illustration, on the whole, biblical illustrations will tend to get a green light for familiarity and interest. Depending on the biblical literacy of the congregation, Bible stories will be familiar. But even if the stories themselves, or the customs and culture, are not familiar, the issues they address often are.[15]

---

15. "Character studies can be used as illustrations or the basis for sermon topics. Presenting biblical characters also helps modern audiences identify with individuals who, like themselves, have families to raise, careers to build, governments to serve, and relationships with the Lord to maintain." House, "Preaching in the Historical Books," 290.

Bible stories are also interesting. They have the capacity to captivate an audience as much as, if not more than, any other story. The effectiveness characteristics that will need intensified scrutiny are clarity and appropriateness.

Be clear. As with other types of illustrations, preachers need to avoid including extraneous or inaccurate details in their biblical illustrations so they will function to help the congregation members understand, apply, or experience the text. Preachers must keep the text in front of them as they are writing the illustrations to make sure they are accurately depicting what the text says, and if they make editorial comments along the way, it should be clear to the audience what material is biblical and what material is the preacher's commentary. The nature of the source material—that it is authoritative—requires special considerations. Not only does the illustration need to parallel the text being illustrated, but the story needs to be making the same point that the text makes (an observation that I will address in a moment).

Be appropriate. Certainly, Bible stories are appropriate to include in a sermon, but not all biblical stories are appropriate for every preaching occasion. Preachers will likely not use an illustration on Mother's Day based on the two mothers discussing which of their babies they should eat first (2 Kgs 6:28–30). Neither would they illustrate a baby dedication sermon from the imprecatory psalm that speaks of taking the Babylonian captors' babies and dashing their heads against the rocks (Ps 137). All of God's word is inspired and inerrant, but not every passage is appropriate as a basis for a biblical illustration.

Drawing on the strengths mentioned by the champions of biblical illustrations, and listening respectfully to the dissenting voices, preachers can use biblical illustrations to assist congregation members in understanding, applying, or experiencing the text. Because of the unique, authoritative nature of their source material, they require the following special considerations.

Ensure the point of the story mirrors the sermon's point. In a sermon posted on sermons.faithlife.com entitled "The Seven Deadly Sins: Lust," the anonymous author begins with a biblical illustration that fails to carry the point of the biblical narrative into the sermon it was supposed to illustrate because it lists Samson's chief character flaw as an inability to "get a handle on his lust."[16] In my view, the sermon illustration fails to adequately summarize Samson's flaws. Samson's problem was not limited to lust, neither was it his primary flaw. Commentator Rob Fleenor agrees:

> Modern commentators offer diverse assessments of Samson's character based on the extensive biographical treatment he receives in the book of Judges. For example:
>
> • Wilson describes Samson as immature and developmentally stunted in his masculinity (Wilson, "Samson the Man-Child," 43–60).
>
> • Niditch views Samson as a hero akin to Robin Hood (Niditch, "Samson as Culture Hero," 621–24).
>
> • Frolov casts Samson as a punishing hero willing to cruelly humiliate his opponents in retaliation for their offenses against Israel (Frolov, *Judges*, 265–69).
>
> • Schipper argues that Samson is arrogantly confident in his abilities (Schipper, "What Was Samson Thinking," 61–67).

---

16. Anonymous, "The Seven Deadly Sins: Lust," https://sermons.faithlife.com/sermons/114889-the-seven-deadly-sins:-lust.

These diverse assessments reveal attempts to discern how ancient readers viewed Samson as both a divine emissary and a practical antihero. Ultimately, Samson is viewed as both a great and flawed hero.[17]

In Fleenor's summary of commentators' views, notably absent is lust as Samson's primary character flaw. Like others whom Fleenor summarizes, scholar J. C. Moyer sees Samson's life as both positive and negative. On the negative side, he disobeyed God and did not keep his vow, but on the positive side, he is a hero of the faith because God used him to defeat his enemy. Moyer writes, "Samson broke his Nazirite vow and disobeyed God, and therein is his religious significance. His life is a negative example of a charismatic leader who came to a tragic, yet heroic, end. Nevertheless, his partial victory over the enemy was reason to be named with the heroes of the faith (Heb 11:32)."[18]

This instance is straightforward; the biblical illustration lacks the needed clarity because the point of the narrative does not match the point the preacher is attempting to illustrate. The illustration not only weakens the preacher's credibility with a biblically literate listener, but it also fogs the points the preacher was attempting to make. Certainly, lust is a problem. But instead of shaping a Bible story to fit the preacher's conviction, the preacher could have used another type of illustration, like this one:

> Dayton Moore is the general manager of the Kansas City Royals. He is battling to educate his young players on the harm pornography does both to the players themselves and to the women they love. Surprisingly, he is getting

---

17. Fleenor, "Samson the Judge: Critical Issues."
18. Moyer, "Samson," 252.

pushback, not from the team but from people in the porn industry, some sports journalists, and some scientists.

Moore uses Fight the New Drug (FTND), a nonreligious anti-porn organization to help educate the younger players about "the harmful effects of pornography" and the need to honor women, respecting them as human beings and not as sexual objects.

In an era when powerful men are falling from grace due to sexual misconduct toward women, the church needs to stand with Moore, teaching young men how to view and treat women properly.[19]

In my view, this is a clear-cut call. Samson's greatest problem was not lust. However, not every determination is as clear—often it is a judgment call that comes down to how the preacher sees the authorial intent of the passage.

For instance, in his sermon "Stress/Worry/Anxiety and the Christian Life," Ernie Arnold uses back-to-back biblical illustrations to demonstrate the role prayer plays in reducing stress, worry, and anxiety. He begins the sermon with a fictional illustration adapted from Haddon Robinson's book *What Jesus Said About Successful Living* and several statistics about the harm stress does in people's lives. After exposing several myths about stress, he wraps up his introduction with the following:

> To answer all of that, I want to share with you this morning five simple things that all of us can do to help us with our times of stress, worry, and anxiety. All of these come from Scripture. Five simple steps that we can all do no matter if we are 5 or 105. Five simple steps that will enable

---

19. Jim L. Wilson and Rodger Russell, "A MLB Executive Fights Porn," https://sermons.faithlife.com/sermons/289968-a-mlb-executive-fights-porn.

us to grow as humans and as disciples of Jesus. Five simple things that we can do to find a balance in our lives.

He provides two illustrations for his first point, "The first and most important thing we can do is to simply go to the Lord in prayer." One of the illustrations features Elisha and his servant:

> In 2 Kings 6:17, Elisha and his servant find themselves under a great deal of stress. They are surrounded by an army of men who have been sent to kill them. Elisha's servant is overwhelmed with worry and anxiety. Who wouldn't be? I mean, if there were a small army that had been sent to take your head, wouldn't you be a little stressed out? Wouldn't you be a little anxious?
>
> Elisha lifts up his voice in prayer, and suddenly, God is there as his Almighty partner. Elisha asks God to allow his young servant to see what he was already seeing. All around Elisha was a company of angels ready to do battle for him and for the boy. Your stress level can fall when you realize that you have a company of angels getting ready to do battle for you. Your stress level can fall when you connect with God, when you partner with God.
>
> All of that happened because Elisha went to prayer. All of that happened because Elisha connected with God and realized that in God and with God, nothing is impossible.[20]

Was Elisha's prayer out of concern for his servant's anxiety, or was it because he wanted his servant to be a man of faith? If you answer that it was because of his anxiety, then the illustration is

---

20. Ernie L. Arnold, "Stress/Worry/Anxiety and the Christian Life," https://sermons.faithlife.com/sermons/126191-stressworryanxiety-and-the-christian-life.

appropriate. However, if you answer that it was so he would grow in his faith, or any other reason, then it would not be appropriate to use as an illustration for a sermon on reducing anxiety.

While this is a judgment call, it is not subjective. Remember, when we use biblical narratives as sermon illustrations, we are using a sacred source. With every other type of illustration, the story just needs to be parallel, but with biblical illustrations, preachers are handling the text and cannot force them where they do not belong. Just as responsible expository preachers would never twist a Scripture to make a point, they cannot shape a biblical story to make a point that it does not make, even when the demands of ministry put pressure on the preacher to do so.

The preacher's schedule is relentless. Sunday morning comes every 152 hours. Every preacher knows the pressure of finding time to do everything that needs to be done, including sermon preparation. One of the pressures is to find good illustrations that help the congregation understand, apply, or experience the text. It is tempting to use whatever personal or biblical story comes to mind. But using a biblical story requires taking the extra time to consider authorial intent and discover the point of the narrative.

Tell the whole story. In "James 3:13–18 (Earthly Wisdom vs. Godly Wisdom)," an unknown author abbreviates a story by inserting "You know how the story goes" in the truncated illustration. The preacher says:

> Both Lot and Abraham had large herds of cattle, and their herdsmen quarreled over their pasturelands. In his wisdom, Abraham suggested that the two separate. Being the godly man he was, he gave Lot his choice of land. The Bible tells that Lot chose the lush, fertile, land of the Jordan River valley. The pasture may have looked better, but Lot failed to consider the consequences when he "pitched his tent

toward Sodom" (Gen 13:12). You know how the story goes. As a result of Lot's unwise decision, he lost everything he had except his two daughters. Even his wife turned back to look and in doing so turned into a pillar of salt.[21]

In reviewing my published sermons, I noticed that I often do the same thing. I assume that people in the audience know the story, and I rush through it. For example, in the sermon "Immutability of God," based on James 1:17, I refer to multiple biblical stories:

> He doesn't change, but the way he's revealed himself to us has changed throughout time. Hebrews 1:1–3 says, "God, who at various times and in various ways spoke in time past to the fathers by the prophets, has in these last days spoken to us by His Son, whom He has appointed heir of all things, through whom also He made the worlds; who being the brightness of His glory and the express image of His person, and upholding all things by the word of His power, when He had by Himself purged our sins, sat down at the right hand of the Majesty on high" (NJJV).
>
> To Adam and Eve, he was a voice walking in the garden, seeking his fallen creation (Gen 3:8). To Moses, he was a voice thundering out of a burning bush that was not consumed by the fire (Exod 3:2–6). To Manoah and his wife, God was a flame ascending into heaven from the altar (Judg 13:20–22). To Moses, Aaron, and Miriam, he was a pillar of cloud, standing in the tabernacle door (Num 12:4–8). Isaiah saw him in a vision, sitting on his throne

---

21. Anonymous, "James 3:13–18 (Earthly Wisdom vs. Godly Wisdom)," https://sermons.faithlife.com/sermons/114197-james-3_13–18 -(earthly-wisdom-vs-godly-wisdom).

in glory (Isa 6:1). Ezekiel saw him in a whirlwind (Ezek 1). Jacob saw him in a dream (Gen 28:12–13). The children of Israel saw him in pillars of clouds (Exod 14:19).

In the beginning of the first century, he revealed himself in the person of Jesus Christ. John 1:14 says, "And the Word became flesh and dwelt among us, and we beheld His glory, the glory as of the only begotten of the Father, full of grace and truth" (NKJV), and 1 John 1:1 says, "That which was from the beginning, which we have heard, which we have seen with our eyes, which we have looked upon, and our hands have handled, concerning the Word of life" (NKJV).

Today, he reveals himself through his written word and the work of the Holy Spirit. He's revealed himself in different ways throughout the ages, but he hasn't changed.[22]

Unfortunately, this clustering of biblical narratives will only be meaningful for biblically literate people. It ignores the fact that some in the congregation will be hearing the stories for the first time. Some listeners have little to no church background, and when we rush through a story, they will get lost. While it is important to avoid extraneous and inaccurate details, it is also important to include enough details for the listeners to experience the full impact of the story. I wonder if it would have been a better idea to provide more details for one or two of the stories, even if it meant referencing fewer stories.

Don't spiritualize the events of the narrative. One of the pitfalls of preaching biblical narratives is to spiritualize the details of the narrative instead of following the plot dynamics to the point.

---

22. Jim L. Wilson, "Immutability of God," https://sermons.faithlife.com/sermons/803760-immutability-of-god

For instance, many preachers have heard (or preached) sermons on 1 Samuel 17 that speak of "how to defeat the giants in your life." The point of that narrative is not to help the readers learn to cope with their "giants"—depression, financial instability, failing health, etc.—nor is it intended as a metaphor for people facing impossible odds. It functions in the narrative to show the movement of God's blessing from the tragic life of a disobedient king to the future king who is a man after God's own heart. Specifically, the narrative episode shows that God uses people who place their trust in him to accomplish his purposes, care for his people, and bring him glory.

Unfortunately, preachers often miss that in every biblical narrative, God is the main character, and the other characters, both heroic and tragic, are merely the supporting cast. First Samuel 17 is about God who accomplishes his purposes, not about how he helps people accomplish their goals. While overcoming depression, regaining financial equilibrium, and enjoying good health are all good things, they are not the point of this narrative episode.

Another common way preachers spiritualize biblical narratives is when they refer to literal storms, like the one God sent on the ship carrying Jonah to Tarshish, or the storm that overtook the disciples on the Sea of Galilee, as illustrations of the kinds of suffering that come into our lives.[23]

But in both cases, these were real storms, not "storms of life." They were not analogous with suffering and pain. Avoid this common pitfall when you preach on narrative passages and when you use them as sermon illustrations.

As they should, preachers often use biblical illustrations to help members of their congregations understand, apply, or

---

23. Dan Shapley, "02 Satan-The Destroyer," https://sermons.faithlife.com/sermons/14147–02-satan-the-destroyer.

experience the text. They have their advantages. They are easy to find, are familiar to many members of the congregation, and have an authority like no other kind of illustration. However, they require special attention to make sure they are used appropriately.

As with all illustration types, preachers should evaluate them before using them to make sure they are familiar, clear, interesting, and appropriate. Most often, they are green-lighted for familiarity and the level of interest most listeners will have in them. While common sense will guide most preachers in making appropriate selections, they need to give special attention to clarity—paying close attention to whether their chosen illustrations illustrate the point in the sermon.

When used well, biblical illustrations have the added benefits of promoting biblical literacy, exposing the congregation members to a fuller range of biblical material, and being able to speak authoritatively, not merely shining a light on the text.

7

Hypothetical and Historical Illustrations

A good sermon does not write itself. Sermon preparation is hard work. The exegetical demands alone are daunting—not just because of the difficulty of proper exegesis and the quest for locating the author's intent, but also because of the necessity of communicating a timeless message from ancient literature to contemporary audiences, which requires locating illustrations that build bridges from then to now. Illustrations—good ones—are not sermon fillers; they help congregation members understand, apply, or experience the text. Finding just the right one is exhilarating. Not being able to find one is frustrating.

So, what if you have scoured your usual sources and you cannot find one? You've racked your brain for a Bible story or a personal experience and come up empty. Maybe you get so desperate that you're even willing to use a canned illustration this week. So, you locate the anthology of illustrations on the shelf, blow the dust off the book, but still come up empty.

Instead of making up a story (chapter 8 deals with fictional illustrations), you could write a hypothetical illustration that will pose a series of what-if questions or provides hypothetical examples. Preaching professor James Cox recommends using hypothetical illustrations when you cannot find an appropriate sermon illustration that actually happened, writing, "The hypothetical example offers a way of exemplifying an idea for which we do not have an appropriate specific instance, whether historical or personal."[1]

Hypothetical Illustrations

While they are a viable option when you cannot locate an appropriate illustration, they also can be an attractive alternative to overusing personal stories, references to pop culture, or historical events. In each of these cases, overuse could cause an imbalance between the primary and secondary functions. If you talk about yourself too much, your narrative can overtake the text and put the spotlight on you. The same can happen with frequent references to sporting events, pop culture, or historical stories. Variety helps keep the focus on the text, not on you or anything else. Mixing it up will help keep your sermons from becoming predictable.

Preachers in our study group used hypothetical illustrations enough to earn them a spot in the frequently used cluster. They work particularly well to introduce a sermon.[2] In his sermon "The Gospel According to Exodus," Barrett Case uses a hypothetical illustration to introduce four proper responses to the gospel:

Think about how you respond to various events:

At a local basketball game, our response is to stand and cheer, or maybe to yell at the referee …

When someone asks, "Will you marry me?" the hopeful response is "Yes, yes, a thousand times yes!"

---

1. Cox, *Preaching*, 209.

2. Mayhue, "Introductions, Illustrations, and Conclusions," 245.

When the officer pulls you over, comes up to your window, and asks, "Do you know why I pulled you over?" the typical response is, "No, officer. I have no idea. Everything okay?"

When you hear the Good News of Jesus Christ, when you think about what God has done for you, there are several proper responses … [3]

Note that he provides three common situations. The first one would relate to a broad cross section of the congregation. People could easily substitute any other sporting event for a basketball game and could see themselves responding to what is happening in the event. The second one would especially relate to young people looking forward to a proposal but also to those who have already been involved in that watershed conversation. The third is another instance common to many. If a listener did not relate to the first three, they would insert their own common event. The three instances form an inclusive pattern that sparks imagination. This is the secondary function of hypothetical illustrations: they prompt the imagination. The repetitive stanzas invite everyone to see themselves in the situation, drawing them in.

Two downsides of hypothetical illustrations are that they do not move an audience the way an actual story will move them,[4] and they are not based in fact—they are not about something that

---

3. Barrett Case, "The Gospel According to Exodus," https://sermons. faithlife.com/sermons/243260-response.

4. "Illustrations will connect with a variety of people if they speak about real human situations. I try not to use hypothetical illustrations—'If I were fired, I would …'—because, though they show the relevant application, they never quite touch the heart." Hestenes, "Not Everyone Learns Alike," 52–53.

actually happened—which can work against credibility.[5] However, if they are about believable situations that are easy for the congregation to relate to, they can prepare the people to listen. In effect, they create an atmosphere for the gospel proclamation that follows.

Hypothetical illustrations are not just an option for when preachers cannot find an appropriate illustration based in fact or an alternative to overusing other types of sermon illustrations. Sometimes, hypothetical illustrations are the best choice. They are especially helpful when a preacher needs to introduce a delicate topic.

Hypothetical illustrations provide an indirect way to surface an issue. In his sermon "Christian Liberty (part 2)," Brian Braddock illustrates God's intention to have "unity with diversity" by asking the audience to imagine a created world without diversity:

> God loves to put diverse things together in such a way that they unite in glorifying him without demanding that they be identical in every way. And aren't you glad he does it that way? Imagine if every bird sang the same song or [donned] the same plumage! Imagine if every tree had the same leaves, or every person shard the same voice. That would indeed be unity … but unity without diversity would be so dull, unengaging, boring. Unity without diversity would be awful!
>
> But God's desire for unity with diversity doesn't just apply to the created universe we see today. God desires

---

5. "While someone can argue or doubt a hypothetical situation, a true account 'proves' its point." Galli and Larson, *Preaching that Connects*, 76.

unity and diversity throughout his kingdom and throughout eternity.[6]

After introducing the concept of what a world would be like
without diversity, he reads Revelation 5:9–10 and asks the people
to imagine what a church could be like with diversity:

> Imagine the diversity in a church with people from every
> tribe, nation, and language. Imagine what kind of differ-
> ences exist in a church filled with people from many dif-
> ferent cultures! Differences in styles and preferences, in
> clothing, food, music. (I've been a member of a multilin-
> gual church, and we had unity!)
>
> What the church looks like today should be moving
> more and more toward what it will be for eternity. A
> diverse, multicultural church is a microcosm of what the
> church will ultimately be. [7]

Braddock had several ways he could have introduced the
topic. He could have used a historical illustration, like Dr. Martin
Luther King Jr.'s 1960 statement on *Meet the Press*: "Eleven o'clock
on Sunday morning is one of the most segregated hours if not the
most segregated hour of Christian America."[8] Or he could have
told the Bible story of Paul confronting Peter for his hypocrisy in
treating gentile Christians differently when his Jewish friends were
around (Gal 2:11–21). Both of these illustrations parallel the text
well. However, they both are better suited for a conclusion than
an introduction. They sum up the teaching well, but they do not

---

6. Brian Braddock, "Christian Liberty (part 2)," https://sermons.faithlife.
com/sermons/269622-christian-liberty-part-2.

7. Braddock, "Christian Liberty (part 2)."

8. *Meet the Press*, April 17, 1960, https://www.youtube.com/watch?v
=1q881g1L_d8.

provoke imagination and exploration. Illustrations that present the final word should be at the end of a thought, not the beginning. Remember, not every suitable illustration works in every location of the sermon (see chapter 3). In this case, Braddock's choice was likely the best one.

Hypothetical illustrations provide case studies to examine. Hypothetical illustrations can be the homiletical equivalent of teachers using case studies in the classroom.[9] They invite the congregation to pause for a moment to reflect theologically and align their current practice to "their best understanding of God's truth."[10] In the sermon "What Makes Grace So Amazing," Dennis McGowan uses a hypothetical illustration to invite members of his congregation into deep reflection about how their family-of-origin experiences influence how they view God, and then he invites them to view God according to scriptural teachings

> But although grace is critically important, it's also scarce. For example, perhaps you grew up in a home where grace was largely absent. What you heard from one or both of your parents was that nothing you ever did was good enough. You could never perform well enough to gain their approval and acceptance. It's not that your parents didn't love you. More than likely, they thought they were doing the right thing by withholding praise and heaping on the criticism; they thought they were helping prepare you for life by emphasizing your flaws and failures instead of your achievements and successes. Or maybe they were just repeating what their parents had taught them. But regardless, what you learned was that you're not

---

9. Brown, et al., *Steps to the Sermon*, 130.

10. Wilson and Waggoner, *A Guide to Theological Reflection*, 23.

good enough. And when that kind of message gets burned into your mind during childhood, it's awfully hard to erase.

Or you may come from a church background in which God's grace was never mentioned. Instead, God was presented as a harsh, demanding taskmaster who would accept nothing less than flawless obedience. Instead of delighting in the lives of his people, he spent all of his time sitting on his throne, looking down on the earth, waiting for them to mess up. Then, with an angry scowl, he would punish them with some terrible misfortune. Or he would mark their transgression down in his book, keeping track of their sins to condemn them at the Day of Judgment. And if you messed up badly enough, you would lose your salvation. You would be rejected by God, cast out, and banished.

What do these types of experiences and ideas produce? They produce people who feel like they're on a performance treadmill with God. And people who feel like they can never gain God's approval, no matter what they do, no matter how fast they run or how hard they work. They become people who feel rejected by God; people who are full of pain and shame; people who struggle with anger, and fear, and anxiety.

The good news is that these are distortions of the truth about God, not the reality. The good news is that God's acceptance of us is completely unconditional. His love is offered freely and without cost. His favor toward us is given without respect to merit or demerit, worth or worthlessness, accomplishment or failure. We cannot earn God's approval or his forgiveness, and the good news is that we don't have to. Our behavior, good or bad, has absolutely no effect on God's attitude toward us. We can't cause him to love us more by being good or make him love us less by being bad. His love for us, his affection toward us, and his acceptance of us are perfect and unchanging. [11]

This case study approach could not only serve as a corrective for their applied theology, but it could also produce greater emotional health. The hypothetical illustration prepares the people to receive instruction about who God really is and challenges them to view him correctly.

Hypothetical illustrations are inclusive. Some illustrations appeal only to sports fans. Other illustrations have special appeal to those who love the opera or have an interest in the arts. The problem is that they invite some people to the table and exclude others. One of the strengths of hypothetical illustrations is they are inclusive; they appeal to a broad swath of the audience. In his sermon "Growing When the Going Gets Tough (1 Pet 4:12–19)" the preacher invites everyone to reflect on what it means to go through hard times with a hypothetical illustration:

> Christians are not exempt from hard times, especially if these times come just because they are Christians. Some believers struggle hard to work with integrity but then get bypassed on the promotion, which is instead given to the guy who has integrity issues. Sometimes we invest hours in someone's life to get them grounded in the Lord, but they turn around and slander us. Or we may not suffer for being a Christian, but we may still suffer. You try to take care of your body but are faced with one health issue after another, while some unbelievers you know abuse their body and do not seem to be suffering one bit. Or your only child you have prayed years for finally arrives

---

11. Dennis McGowan, "What Makes Grace So Amazing," https://sermons.faithlife.com/sermons/89882-what-makes-grace-so-amazing.

but is then diagnosed with leukemia at the age of three. It doesn't make sense sometimes, actually most, if not all of the time.[12]

Historical Illustrations

Most of the illustration types in the infrequently used cluster will appear in the next chapter. However, we will look at historical illustrations in this chapter to give them heightened attention. Of those in the infrequently used cluster, historical illustrations have the greatest possibility for effectiveness, especially if the congregation members are highly educated and share a common interest in classical literature or history.[13]

Certainly, historical illustrations can be clear, interesting, and appropriate to use[14]—what makes them less popular than those in the frequently used cluster is that their subject matter will be familiar to fewer people. Because they are not familiar, they will likely take longer to tell and may need some additional clarification to establish their relevance to the audience before showing their relevance to the text.

If it is "not likely that any members in the congregation will be familiar with, know about, identify with, or have a connection

---

12. Scott Brockett, "Growing When the Going Gets Tough (1 Pet 4:12–19)," https://sermons.faithlife.com/sermons/752617-untitled-sermon.

13. "Are historical illustrations out? No. They deal with what has happened, not what might happen. They are about fact, not fiction. Also, many people love history. And sometimes the best illustration is one that happened thirty years ago, not last week. What happened matters. When it happened isn't always important." Moyer, *Show Me How to Illustrate Evangelistic Sermons,* 24.

14. "Sermons—and congregations—would be well served by illustrations that include not just personal stories and popular culture elements like film clips and the omnipresent sports story but also the force of great novels and plays and the texts of great poems." de Rosset, "Felling the Devil," 240–41.

with the illustration,"[15] an illustration should be red-lighted. However, in the case of historical illustrations, the benefits of the secondary function might be high enough that they are worth the extra time and effort to connect them with the audience and the text.

Illustrations from church history. Randy Adams, who teaches Proclamation and Worship with me in Gateway Seminary's Doctor of Ministry program, is a proponent of including historical illustrations in sermons. He is successful in using them due in large part to his knack for helping his audience identify and connect with the events featured in the illustration. In his sermon "The Cost of Missions," preached at Oklahoma Baptist University Missions Week Chapel in 2012, he uses several historical illustrations to provide a context for future decisions the students would be making. He begins the sermon with a fresh illustration about the life and death of Cheryl Harvey, a missionary in Jordan who had been martyred only eight days before.

After securing their attention with this opening illustration, and before transitioning to his assigned text, Psalm 67, he places the recent events into the historical context of his audience's ancestors. Notice how he establishes the connection between the historical event and the audience.

> And it's only right that we send missionaries to people who don't know Jesus, and that we go ourselves, because you and I are here today because someone sent a missionary-evangelist to us or our people, and it cost them greatly to do so. How many of you all have a background

---

15. "Preachers have always made much use of illustration from History. The field is in itself boundless, but is in practice greatly limited by the popular lack of extensive acquaintance with it." Broadus, *A Treatise on the Preparation and Delivery of Sermons*, 236.

in England? Your ancestors. Like the Pilgrims. Me too. Did you know our ancestors were barbaric, dangerous people? Many suffered taking the gospel of Jesus Christ to the Anglo-Saxons in England 1,500 years ago.

By the way, did you know that hundreds of years before there was a church in England, there were churches in Ethiopia? One of the greatest church buildings in the world is in Istanbul, Turkey—the Hagia Sophia. It was built when Istanbul was the Christian city of Constantinople. Today, Turkey is the least Christian country in the world; there are four to five thousand Christians out of seventy million people. But there's a tremendous church building in Turkey that was built more than sixty years before the missionary evangelists traveled to England and founded the church. The oldest church building in England is St. Martin's Church in Canterbury, built in 597. There are church buildings in Syria, the Republic of Georgia, Egypt, France, Germany, the Netherlands, older than England. There are older churches in Bulgaria, Armenia, and Serbia. In fact, there's a church building in China that's only about forty years younger than the oldest church in England (Nestorian, Xi'an, built in 640).

But the breakthrough in taking the gospel to my ancestors came in the year 596, when forty missionaries … left Rome for Canterbury, England. Gregory the Great, the Roman pontiff, said that England was "the ends of the earth." They didn't want to go. And when they got close, they sent a letter back to Rome saying, please let us come home. But Gregory the Great told them to continue. They were concerned because they'd heard such terrible things about our great-great-great-grandparents. But they went, and God was in it. In less than a year, the English King

Ethelbert himself was converted to Christ. And get this: on Christmas Day in Canterbury, England in AD 597, over ten thousand people were baptized. With that, the church was planted permanently in England.

Similar stories can be told of the Germanic people, many Africans, Koreans, Native Americans, and others the world over. The story of the spread of the gospel of Jesus Christ is the story of missionaries. Missionaries who paid the price. Missionaries who answered the call of God, were sent by the church of God, fulfilling the purpose of God, going back to Old Testament times. We often think of what missionaries have done since the Apostle Paul. But hundreds of years before Jesus was born, God stated His intention to reach peoples from all over the world.[16]

Using historical illustrations required Adams to connect the illustration to the audience (since the people, places, and times mentioned in the illustration were likely unfamiliar to the listeners) before connecting it to the text. The reason I recommend red-lighting illustrations with mostly unfamiliar elements is this need for double connection. Often, they require orienting the audience to two worlds—the world of the text and the world of the illustration. Not only does that absorb time, but it drains interest, making it difficult to make the illustration clear. The exception to the rule is if the double connection can be done quickly. If this would have taken a lot of time, then it would have been better to find a different way to illustrate Psalm 67, but he was able to do it in less than ten seconds by speaking about their ancestors.

---

16. Randy Adams, "The Cost of Missions—OBU Missions Week Chapel," https://sermons.faithlife.com/sermons/499660-the-cost-of-missions-obu-mission's-week-chapel.

In the context of Adams's sermon—missions week at a Christian university in the Bible belt—he likely could not have made a better choice than to use historical illustrations in the body of his sermon. This surfaces an important point for us to consider: the fact that an illustration type is infrequently used by others does not mean it should not be used. The congregational setting and the pastor's personality and interests can justify deviating from the norm.

Secondary function. As with every other type of illustration, historical illustrations have a secondary function. Beyond helping the audience understand, apply, or experience the text, they also provide a needed historical context for practicing the faith. Professor Robert Thomas writes:

> The doctrinal and ethical development of the Christian church from century to century can be evaluated properly only through the eyes of the correctly understood Bible. Lessons learned by earlier generations of believers, both good and bad, make excellent sermon illustrations. They also provoke imitation of exemplary behavior of saints of the past and guard Christians from repeating the mistakes of those who have gone before.[17]

On their own, history lessons are good, just like learning about the pastor's life is good (personal illustrations), seeing how faith intersects with pop culture is good (fresh illustrations), or encouraging imagination is good (hypothetical illustrations), but the primary function of illustrations is to help listeners understand, apply, or experience the text. The secondary function must remain secondary; it cannot overshadow the primary function.

---

17. Thomas, "Exegesis and Expository Preaching," 144.

Using historical material of the church to illustrate a biblical text has the added benefit of teaching church history. Since understanding church history is important to understanding current Christian practice, using such illustrations is warranted as long as they "expand and deepen understanding of a text."[18]

Telling stories from the lives of the giants of the faith also presents people with examples to emulate. Thomas Cornman writes, "Whether dead for hundreds of years, or alive and continuing to live out the gospel, we must not ignore the lives of dedicated Christ-followers in our illustrations."[19]

For instance, preachers often use events from George Mueller's life to illustrate the power of prayer, as Richard Rich does in his sermon "The Power of Persistent Prayer" with this story:

> George Mueller was known for his powerful prayer. In the course of his ministry to the orphans of England, he never asked for financial assistance from men—only God and he constantly received what was needed, to the penny.
>
> Once while on his way to speak in Quebec for an engagement, on the deck of the ship that was to carry him to his destination, he informed the captain that he needed to be in Quebec by Saturday afternoon. The captain related the story: "'It is impossible,' I said. 'Do you know how dense this fog is?'
>
> "'No,' he replied, 'my eye is not on the density of the fog, but on the living God who controls every circumstance

---

18. "Illustrations exegete Scripture in terms of the human condition, creating a whole-person understanding of God's Word. Illustrations are essential to effective exposition not merely because they easily stimulate interest but also because they expand and deepen understanding of a text." Chappell, *Christ-Centered Preaching*, 178.

19. Cornman, "History: The Hidden Gold Mine," 262.

of life. I have never broken an engagement in fifty-seven years; let us go down into the chart room and pray.' He knelt down and prayed one of the simplest prayers. When he had finished, I was going to pray, but he put his hand on my shoulder and told me not to pray. 'As you do not believe he will answer, and as I believe he has, there is no need whatever for you to pray about it.'

"I looked at him, and George Mueller said, 'Captain, I have known my Lord for fifty-seven years, and there has never been a single day when I have failed to get an audience with the King. Get up, Captain, and open the door, and you will find that the fog has gone.'

"I got up and the fog indeed was gone, and on that Saturday afternoon, George Mueller kept his promised engagement."[20]

Similarly, Steve Caswell uses a story about William Booth in his sermon "The Furtherance of the Gospel" to illustrate the desires of the apostles' hearts:

William Booth was too sick to attend an International Salvation Army conference on service. So instead, he sent a telegram to be read at the conference. The large gathering was expecting a stirring challenge to service or evangelism. Instead, it contained only one word, "Others."

The apostles had three desires, and they are all centered in Christ. One was to be found in Christ; another was to

---

20. Richard O. Rich, "The Power of Persistent Prayer," https://sermons.faithlife.com/sermons/52355-the-power-of-persistent-prayer.

magnify Christ; and the third was to be with Christ. We need these same three desires.[21]

While illustrations of people from the past can be helpful, there is a danger of overusing illustrations that feature the same person week after week. Just as preachers need to be careful not to talk about their personal lives too much, and not every fresh illustration should be about Taylor Swift or LeBron James, not every sermon needs to mention Dwight Moody or Charles Spurgeon.

A couple of years ago, I had several students who wove a story or a quote from the Prince of Preachers into every sermon—so much so that it became a distraction. To get them thinking about this issue, I asked them to take what I called the "Spurgeon ten-sermon challenge": to randomly pick any ten Spurgeon sermons and see how often he quoted or told a story of a person (non-Bible character) who was no longer living and who had lived in a country that was foreign to him. I led by example and read ten of Spurgeon's sermons as well, finding only one illustration that fit the criteria. None of my students took me up on the challenge, at least not as far as I know. This was my way of encouraging them to preach *like* Spurgeon but stop preaching *about* Spurgeon.

Stories and notable people from church history (in proper moderation) are effective ways to illustrate biblical truth. That is not to say that preachers should only use historical illustrations based on church history. Preachers can effectively use other stories from history, especially those that do not require time explaining the customs, times, or culture of the people featured in the illustration.

---

21.   Steve Caswell, "The Furtherance of the Gospel Philippians 1c-1," https://sermons.faithlife.com/sermons/114315-the-furtherance-of-the-gospel-philippians-1c-1.

Illustrations from world or national history. Using a historical illustration in a holiday-themed sermon is appropriate. For example, in his sermon "Why Give Thanks," David Krueger alludes to the historical background of Thanksgiving Day in America, quoting William Bradford's 1623 Thanksgiving proclamation, which expressed the colonists' gratitude toward God.[22] Likely, most preachers in the United States have used a similar illustration around the Thanksgiving holiday.

But illustrations from American history do not need to be limited to holidays. In his sermon "Jesus and the Law," Barry Davis uses the following historical story to illustrate his point:

> In the last days of the Civil War, the Confederate capital, Richmond, Virginia, fell to the Union army. Abraham Lincoln insisted on visiting the city. Even though no one knew he was coming, slaves recognized him immediately and thronged around him. He had liberated them by the Emancipation Proclamation, and now, Lincoln's army had set them free. According to Admiral David Porter, an eyewitness, Lincoln spoke to the throng around him:
>
> "My poor friends, you are free—free as air. You can cast off the name of slave and trample upon it. … Liberty is your birthright."
>
> But Lincoln also warned them not to abuse their freedom. "Let the world see that you merit [your freedom]," Lincoln said. "Don't let your joy carry you into excesses. Learn the laws and obey them."
>
> That is very much like the message Jesus gives to those whom he has liberated by his death and resurrection. Jesus

---

22. David Krueger, "Why Give Thanks?," https://sermons.faithlife.com/sermons/120138-why-give-thanks.

gives us our true birthright—spiritual freedom. But that freedom isn't an excuse for disobedience; it forms the basis for learning and obeying God's laws.[23]

Another pastor used an event that occurred on the Great Plains in the nineteenth century to help his congregation experience a future event as depicted in the fifth trumpet in the book of Revelation:

What do locusts do best? Eat vegetation of all kinds. They target an area and absolutely conquer it. Then they fly away, and all that is left is devastation, like a swarm that occurred in the Great Plains in 1874, according to History.net. An estimated 120 billion locusts produced a swarm 1,800 miles long and 100 miles wide—a swath equal to the combined areas of Connecticut, Delaware, Maine, Maryland, Massachusetts, New Hampshire, New Jersey, New York, Pennsylvania, Rhode Island, and Vermont.

When they were done eating, all crops, leaves, grass, the wool off sheep, the harnesses off horses, the paint off wagons, and even the handles off pitchforks—gone. The article says, "They feasted for days, even devouring the clothing and quilts." One woman says that locusts literally ate her clothing right off her back. "I was wearing a dress of white with a green stripe," she recalled. "The grasshoppers settled on me and ate up every bit of the green stripe in that dress before anything could be done about it." The article goes on to say that after the locust invasion, only 10

23. Barry Davis, "Jesus and the Law," https://sermons.faithlife.com/sermons/123388-jesus-and-the-law. He cites as his source James L. Swanson, *Bloody Crimes* (New York: William Morrow, 2010), 46.

percent of the families in Kansas had enough provisions to last through the coming winter.[24]

Even though their subject matter is less familiar to most audiences than references to pop culture are, historical illustrations can effectively help congregation members understand, apply, or experience the text. To do so, preachers must quickly make a connection between the audience and the story, establishing relevance to the listeners and text. Historical illustrations have the added benefit of increasing historical literacy and, in some cases, exposing audience members to church history, which gives them a fuller understanding of biblical theology and how to live the Christian life.

---

24. Pastor Glenn, "The Revelation of Jesus Christ, Part 21: The Fifth Trumpet—The Locusts Are Coming," https://sermons.faithlife.com/ sermons/261605-the-revelation-of-jesus-christ-part-21-9:1-12-the-fifth-trumpet:- the-locusts-are-coming.

Classic Illustrations, Fictional Illustrations, and Object Lessons

While historical illustrations, classic illustrations, fictional illustrations, and object lessons were each much less frequently used than the illustrations in the frequently used cluster, taken as a whole, the infrequently used cluster represented 15 16 percent of illustrations used by preachers in our study group. While they may not be used as often as other illustration types, preachers do use them to help their listeners understand, apply, or experience the text.

Classic Illustrations

Classic illustrations are commonly used older stories. In his sermon on 1 Thessalonians 2:1–12, Robert Ward uses this one:

> A man in the army of Alexander the Great, who was also named Alexander, was accused of cowardly actions. He was brought before Alexander, who asked what his name was.
>
> Not a little intimidated, the man mumbled, "Alexander."
> "I can't hear you," the ruler stated pointedly.

Again, the man replied, but a little louder, "Alexander."

Still not satisfied, the great leader said, "Louder!"

"Alexander," the man almost shouted in fear.

At this, Alexander the Great commented, "Either change your name or change your conduct."[1]

I've used this story too. Perhaps you have also used it, or if you have not, you may have heard it. Another common one is the story of the cook who cut the ends off of the ham before cooking it. In his sermon "The Shepherd and the Stranger," John A. Murphy Jr. uses this often-repeated story to illustrate the tendency people have to unthinkingly imitate others:

> I think all of us can relate to the story of a young married couple preparing to have family over for dinner. The young wife, as she was preparing the ham, cut off the ends, compelling her husband to ask why she was cutting off good meat. She said, "Well, that's the way my mother always did it."
>
> Curious, she called her mom to find out why they cut off the ends of the ham to cook it. Her mom had a similar answer: "That's the way my mom always did it."
>
> Well, it was time to call grandma. So the young woman called her grandma and asked, "Hey grandma, Mom and I both cut off the ends of the ham to cook it. She apparently learned it from you, and I learned it from her. Why do you cut off the ends of the ham to cook it?"

1. Robert Ward, "1 Thessalonians 2:1–12," https://sermons.faithlife.com/sermons/458504–1-thessalonians-2:1–12.

The grandma was very matter of fact: "Well, I don't know why you two do it, but I do it so it will fit into my pan."[2]

A third common classic illustration is the Charles Blondin wheelbarrow story. In his sermon "Fight Fake Faith," Dan Maruyama uses this illustration, acknowledging that it had already been used in the church by another speaker:

I think Brandon may have actually used this illustration before, but there's a guy named The Great Blondin, and back in 1859, he strung a cable across Niagara Falls 160 feet off the water and almost a quarter mile long. He walked back and forth across—he was a tightrope walker—and even pushed a wheelbarrow across it. History tells us that when he came back with the wheelbarrow, he said to the crowd, "Do you believe that I could carry somebody across the falls in this wheelbarrow?" And everyone said, "Yes, definitely. We just saw you walk back and forth seven times!" Then, he said, "So who wants to get in?"[3]

When I did a keyword search at sermons.faithlife.com, I found forty-six sermons with the word "Blondin" in them. Since it is an unusual name, I was pretty sure that all the search results referred to the tightrope walker, but just to make sure, I clicked on every link. While the details varied, they all referred to the Niagara Falls challenge.

---

2. John A. Murphy Jr., "The Shepherd and the Stranger," https://sermons. faithlife.com/sermons/262259-the-shepherd-and-the-stranger.

3. Dan Maruyama, "Fight Fake Faith," https://sermons.faithlife.com/ sermons/399121-fight-fake-faith.

However, the usage is even more widespread than my search indicated because the number above did not include the sermons with a variation of the illustration that fails to mention the tightrope walker's name.[4]

Classic illustrations are common for a reason. The Alexander the Great story nails the relationship between claiming the name of Christ and the importance of living as he lived. The ham story shows how people often do something repeatedly without knowing why they are doing it. The tightrope story clarifies the difference between agreeing with something and really believing in it. If they did not nail the concept so well, they would have been rejected years ago and would not continue to be in common use.

However, that does not mean they deserve to be used frequently. While I will stop short of saying they should not be used at all, I agree with the voices of other preachers and homileticians who say they should not be used often.[5] Nelson Price discourages their use because they make the pastor seem outdated.[6] Paige Patterson says they take away from the pastor's credibility.[7] Greg Scharf is concerned about their relevance.[8]

---

4. See, for example, Tad Wychopen, "Col 2_11_15 The Spiritual Benefits of Salvation," https://sermons.faithlife.com/sermons/47185-col-2_11_15-the-spiritual-benefits-of-salvation.

5. "Avoid using canned, trite, commonplace and overused illustrations." Akin, Curtis, and Rummage, *Engaging Exposition*, loc. 3494.

6. "Canned illustrations can be used only sparingly to be effective. Excessive use betrays the user as not being involved enough personally in contemporary life to draw applicable truths from the listener's world." Price, "Preaching and Church Growth," 489.

7. "Often-used and dated illustrations and dependence on the work of other well-known ministers will quickly erode the ethos of the man of God." Patterson, "Ancient Rhetoric," 21.

8. "Freshness and relevance are the reasons I recommend you don't recycle tired illustrations from books or Web sources." Scharf, *Relational Preaching*, 131.

On the whole, classic illustrations can be as interesting and appropriate as any other type of illustration. However, they present special challenges with familiarity and clarity.

Familiarity. One of the problems with classic illustrations is that those who are deep in the church culture have already heard them, and those who are not familiar with the church culture will likely not relate to them. They tend not to be about things that interest modern listeners.

The ham story, for example, is cute, quaint, and folksy, but not really relevant. We still cook quite a bit in our house, but we are more likely to use the microwave, slow cooker, Foreman grill, or outdoor barbecue than to open an oven door. In multicultural congregations, an illustration about pho, huarache, dim sum, or another dish the audience is more familiar with might be better than one about a ham.

And crowds of people gathering to watch a tightrope walker? I cannot imagine going to watch such an event, and I suspect the days of a crowd gathering for a spectacle like that are over. While people are familiar with Niagara Falls and may have a memory of the circus, the story seems so foreign. Besides, just as takeout is a more common way to eat than it once was, with Netflix and other streaming services there is a trend toward consumption of entertainment at home.[9]

When churches shared a common worldview, it made more sense to recycle a collection of sermon illustrations than it does today.[10] Most churches don't share the same common rural, folksy

---

9. Feldman, "How Netflix Is Changing the Future of Movie Theaters."

10. "Sermons during the high periods [when people share a common worldview] are carefully designed and often feature the same illustrations, illustrations that are stock understandings of particular Christian convictions." Buttrick, *A Captive Voice*, 69.

roots that the church I attended as a child did, and the stories seem out of place to many listeners. Preachers should consider avoiding canned illustrations for the same reason they have introduced fresh worship music. Such stories make the church seem out of touch.

Clarity. Another problem with classic illustrations is that they are often hazy on details because of how often they have been repeated.

While I was clicking on the dozens of sermons that used the Blondin illustration, I noticed a variant in the details about when it happened. Some said thirty-five years ago, while others placed it in the nineteenth century. And the Alexander the Great story may not even have happened.[11] I found the same line attributed in another sermon to Napoleon Bonaparte.[12] Maybe one of the stories is genuine, or maybe neither is authentic, but likely both did not happen.

Details matter. Whatever type of illustrations preachers use, they have to get the facts right or they lose credibility.[13]

Accuracy is important. Greg Scharf puts it this way:

> This practice [recycling tired illustrations] has a surprisingly long history, and no doubt some stories will always get a reaction. Nevertheless, it is better to use the illustrations of others only as a spur to encourage you to find your own word pictures and examples. Draw your examples

---

11. M. J. Mann, "Legends of Alexander," https://thesecondachilles.com/category/legends-of-alexander/.

12. Anonymous, "Walking Worthy of Your Calling," https://sermons.faithlife.com/sermons/21344-walking-worthy-of-your-calling.

13. "If I say something inaccurate in an illustration about airplanes, the pilots and aircraft hobbyists in the congregation will downgrade everything else I say." Palmer, "Preparing Yourself to Teach," 41.

from your listeners' circumstances, not from times and places as foreign to them as the world of the Bible itself. If a story can be verified and truly sheds light on your text, use it, but always attribute it to your source. If it cannot be verified, acknowledge that it may be apocryphal.[14]

Knowing that some question the accuracy of an illustration highlights the relevance of Scharf's advice. If you were to use the Alexander the Great illustration, you would need to introduce it by saying, "While I cannot vouch for its authenticity, I heard a story that makes this point well."

If a story is fictional, make sure the audience knows it is fictional. Do not claim historicity for something without reasonable assurance that it happened. This raises the question of whether preachers should use outright fictional stories to illustrate.

Fictional Illustrations

A fictional illustration is a made-up story (sometimes called a "preacher's story"), like this one:

> A six-year-old girl once asked her father, "What do you have to do to become a doctor?"
>
> Her father said, "You have to do extremely well in school, take a lot of math and science, get into an excellent college, make the highest grades possible, and then go to medical school, and follow that with an internship. Then you can start your own practice. Honey, as smart as you are, you can be anything you want to be."

---

14. Scharf, *Relational Preaching*, 131–32.

The little girl thought about that and then asked, "What do you have to do to be queen?"[15]

Cute story, right? Or how about this one:

The local news station was interviewing an eighty-year-old lady because she had just gotten married—for the fourth time.

The interviewer asked her questions about her life, about what it felt like to be marrying again at eighty, and then about her new husband's occupation.

"He's a funeral director," she answered.

"Interesting," the newsman thought. He then asked her if she wouldn't mind telling him a little about her first three husbands and what they did for a living.

She paused for a few moments, needing time to reflect on all those years. After a short time, a smile came to her face and she answered proudly, explaining that she'd first married a banker when she was in her early twenties; then a circus ringmaster when in her forties; later on, a preacher when in her sixties; and now in her eighties, a funeral director.

The interviewer looked at her, quite astonished, and asked why she had married four men with such diverse careers.

She smiled and explained, "I married one for the money, two for the show, three to get ready, and four to go."[16]

15. Rich DeRuiter, "I Can Do All Things," https://sermons.faithlife.com/sermons/47637-i-can-do-all-things.

16. Thomas Bevers, "One for the Money, Two for the Show," https://sermons.faithlife.com/sermons/73175-one-for-the-money-two-for-the-show.

While they both may entertain some people in your audience, I would think twice before using either of these illustrations. Both come across as gratuitous. They are either sermon fillers or an attempt to loosen up the listeners with a chuckle before diving into the sermon; either way, they waste precious time. Remember, the only time that preachers have the congregation's full attention is at the beginning of the sermon. The precious opening moments are when people are deciding how seriously they will take the preacher and the message. Those moments should never be trifled away.

However, not all fictional illustrations are intended to be cute or funny; sometimes preachers use them to introduce wisdom, like this one about two monks:

> Two monks were walking through the countryside when they came to the edge of a river. An old woman was sitting there, upset because there was no bridge. The first monk offered to carry her across. The two monks lifted her between them and carried her across the river. When they got to the other side, they set her down, and she went on her way.
>
> After they'd walked another mile or so, the second monk began to complain. "Look at my clothes," he said. "They're filthy from carrying that woman across the river. And my back still hurts from lifting her." The first monk just smiled and nodded his head.
>
> A few minutes later, the second monk griped again, "My back is hurting me so badly, and it is all because we carried that silly woman across the river! I cannot go any farther. But why is it you're not complaining about it, too? Doesn't your back hurt?"

"Of course not," the first monk replied. "You're still carrying the woman, but I set her down five miles ago."

We're often like that second monk. We don't let go of the pain of the past. As a result, we still carry the burdens of things done years ago. As someone has said, "No matter how long you nurse a grudge, it won't get better." And that bitterness damages our lives.[17]

While this story does illustrate the harmful effects of bitterness, I likely would not use it. A glaring issue with fictional stories is, well, they are not true. While, as a group, they could be about familiar things and be interesting and appropriate, I red-light them for clarity because they are not credible.

Contrast the preceding example with these illustrations on the harmful effects of bitterness:

In the 1960s, Simon and Garfunkel was at the top of the recording charts. Then, right at the peak of their popularity, they split up, going their separate musical ways. Now, forty-five years later, we've discovered that Art Garfunkel has never forgiven Paul Simon for the breakup.

Attributing the breakup to Simon's unwillingness to share the spotlight, Garfunkel calls Simon a jerk. He insists that the five-foot-three-inch Simon suffers from a Napoleon complex and says he befriended him in high school out of pity for his small stature. "That compensation gesture," Garfunkel says, "has created a monster."[18]

17. Andrew Burt, "Facing the Giant of Bitterness," https://sermons.faithlife.com/sermons/30754-facing-the-giant-of-bitterness.

18. Jim L. Wilson and Rodger Russell, "Garfunkel Still Has Not Forgiven Paul Simon for Break-Up," https://sermons.faithlife.com/sermons/126067-garfunkel-still-has-not-forgiven-paul-simon-for-break-up.

Does the story about two monks or the one about Garfunkel's struggle have the more authentic feel to you? Another way to illustrate the struggle with bitterness is with an illustration from classic literature.

> In the novel *Wuthering Heights*, Heathcliff, the main character, is treated horribly as a young boy by the Earnshaw family. As he grows older, he plots revenge on those who treated him cruelly and their children—to the point where his vengeance consumes his every thought and action. Isabella, one of the characters who somehow escapes his cruelty, says, "Treachery and violence are spears pointed at both ends—they wound those who resort to them, worse than their enemies." That is exactly what happens to Heathcliff. He dies bitter and alone, while the children of his oppressors live happy, fulfilled lives.[19]

Depending on the congregation, either of these choices works better, in my view, than the fictional illustration. The Garfunkel illustration would be the preference in a congregation in tune with pop culture (of a certain vintage), the *Wuthering Heights* illustration in a congregation more aligned with classic literature.

The issue is that beyond any other type of illustration with a few inaccurate details, the "preacher stories" do not have a ring of truth to them. The issue can be mitigated, to some degree, by acknowledging the stories are fictional. John Broadus wrote at the

---

19. Jim L. Wilson and Abigail Davis, "Classic Novel 'Wuthering Heights' Shows Reality of Bitterness," https://sermons.faithlife.com/sermons/122900 -classic-novel-%22wuthering-heights%22-shows-reality-of-bitterness. There is a difference between illustrations based on a fictional work of art like this novel and fictional illustrations. The novel itself has historical significance. For that reason, I categorize illustrations like this one in the historical illustrations category, which I define as "summarizing an event or character from history or literature."

turn of the twentieth century, "It is perfectly lawful to invent an illustration, even in the form of a story, provided that it possesses verisimilitude, and provided that we either show it to be imaginary, or let nothing depend upon the idea that it is real."[20] But even if a fictional illustration meets Broadus's test, it will always lack the authoritative reality of stories that actually happened.

This is not to say that preachers are not free to use their imaginations to help audiences understand, apply, or experience the text. A better alternative to "preacher stories" is hypothetical illustrations, which pose what-if questions or provide hypothetical examples. Hypothetical illustrations allow preachers to use the full force of their imaginations without stating or implying that the story actually happened. Instead of inviting the audience members to suspend their disbelief, they encourage the people to use their imaginations about how a reasonable person would respond in a specific situation or, better yet, how a person of faith would (should) respond under the circumstances.

Some would cite Jesus's use of parables to justify using fictional stories as sermon illustrations.[21] While Jesus did use examples to teach,[22] they were not stories that he told to merely help his listeners understand, apply, or experience Scripture—they *are* Scripture. This is an important distinction. Jeffrey Arthurs writes, "Parables are not illustrations throwing light on some

---

20. Broadus, *A Treatise on the Preparation and Delivery of Sermons*, 233–34.

21. "Some argue that Jesus' parables are teaching stories that use masterful sermon illustrations to make difficult theological ideas clear and easy to understand. Seen in this light, Jesus is a skillful teacher who used parables to make his instruction clear, forceful, and memorable for his listeners." Fallon, "The Bible Preaches on the Bible," 297–98.

22. "Luther points out that Scripture itself uses examples to teach, such as when Jesus tells parables." Reinis, "Exempla," 267.

abstract truth. The parable is the truth."[23] While drawing lessons from Jesus's teaching to influence our own preaching is a noble pursuit, it is crucial not to make the mistake of categorizing parables as analogous to illustrations.

Preachers will lose credibility with their primary audience if they tell a story that did not happen as if it did. They will also diminish their standing with them by using doctored, cheesy, made-up stories. However, the fallout is not contained to those sitting in the church gathering. Consider for a moment what happens with the secondary and tertiary audiences. Many in the secondary audience, those who watch or listen to the message online, will not know the preacher and will be less inclined to grant the benefit of the doubt, resulting in a diminished view of the preacher, the church, and maybe even the message. The tertiary audience, those who hear about the sermon later from someone who heard it, will be even less generous to the preacher and church.

Equally daunting is if a member of the primary audience believes the veracity of the "preacher story" and repeats it to unbelieving friends. Now the implausibility spreads like gangrene and lessens everybody's credibility.

The preachers in our study group used very few fictional illustrations, which I see as a positive trend. If used at all, they should be used sparingly and should be clearly identified as fictional.

Object Lessons

An object lesson includes the use of a physical object, diagram, or image that is in the preacher's hand or pointed to by the preacher while illustrating the point.

---

23. Arthurs, *Preaching with Variety*, 12.

I suspect that if I had conducted this research twenty years ago, the use of object lessons would have been higher than the 1 percent in our study group. Because of the increased emphasis on creativity at the turn of the millennium, preachers were using props and object lessons in sermons, outside of their regular use during children's church messages. For instance, at one church I attended during that era, the ushers gave me a stone to hold during the sermon. The preacher's text that day was John 8:7. As he dismissed the congregation, the preacher asked us to leave the stone with the ushers as a symbol of our willingness to forsake a judgmental spirit and not "cast the first stone." Another time, I heard a preacher illustrate John 12:24–25 by shucking an ear of corn on the stage to show the number of kernels that had come from a single kernel.

Even if preachers are not creative geniuses, they can incorporate object lessons into their sermons. Some object lessons are as simple as baking some cookies, like this one:

> Has anybody ever told you that something tasted good? What? Have you ever tried it and found out that you didn't like it? Cauliflower, beets …
>
> Well, I have to tell you that I made cookies last night, and boy, are they good! (Eat one.) These are chocolate chip cookies. Don't these look like good cookies?
>
> Can you tell by looking at them that they are good?
>
> Can you tell by smelling them that they are good?
>
> Tasting them is the only sure way to find out. Let's see. Are they good?
>
> Knowing Jesus is the same way. I can tell you about him and show you his love. But the only sure way to know if Jesus is good is if you find out for yourself. Psalm 34:8

says, "Taste and see that the Lord is good." This means try him out. Just like we did the cookies.[24]

I noticed that the illustration included the instruction to eat one. I also noticed that it did not instruct the preacher to pass the plate to others in the audience, but there was a point between the words "Let's see," the question, "Are they good?" and the closing words, "Just like we did the cookies," that leads me to believe that the people actually got to eat a cookie.

What a novel idea. If the logistics were not overwhelming (How big was the congregation? How many cookies did it take? Who passed them out?), if there were no health code violations, and if it didn't wreck anyone's diet, then it sounds like a winner. Roy DeBrand advocates for object lessons:

> Often we explain, illustrate, or apply truth in a sermon by talking about some object, any object which can be used to get the point across. Instead of merely talking about it, why not actually take the object with you and show it while referring to it? Some do this regularly in children's sermons. It need not be limited to children's sermons, however. Objects can be a strong reinforcement to truth in any sermon.[25]

DeBrand asks a good question: why not have the object with you? Below is another object lesson that is a little more involved than passing around a plate of homemade cookies.

Object Lesson: Use three clear glasses. The first should be filled with red wine or grape juice. The second should be

---

24. Bryan O. Clements, "Taste and See That the Lord Is Good," https://sermons.faithlife.com/sermons/17279-taste-and-see-that-the-lord-is-good.

25. DeBrand, "The Visual in Preaching," 405.

empty. The third should be empty and broken or punctured so that it will leak. Tell your listeners that the three glasses represent three hearts. The first (juice) is already filled to overflowing with rich things. The second is empty but still rigid and proud. The last is both empty and broken by the trials and sorrows of this life. Show your listeners a bottle of olive oil and say it represents gifts and power as conveyed by the Holy Spirit. (1) Pour a little olive oil into the wine-filled glass, comment on how little room there is for God's gifts, and point out how they won't mingle with the rich things already there. The gift of God becomes a superficial layer that never penetrates to the depths of that heart. (2) Pour oil into the empty glass and point out that there is room to receive the oil, but that heart is a dead end for those blessings. The empty but proud heart is willing to receive and hoard, but the blessings will spoil over time. (3) Pour oil into the empty and broken glass (make sure to have something underneath to catch the leaks). Explain that an empty, broken heart pleases God since it must receive more of him daily and always leaks his blessings out to others.[26]

The simplicity and straightforward nature of the cookie illustration is not carried over with this object lesson. Not only does it take a great deal of advance preparation, but also, the analogies are not clear—there is not a parallel between the moral being taught and the different containers.

26. C. J. Walker, "Hope for the Holidays (Lk. 1:39–45)," https://sermons. faithlife.com/sermons/336762-sunday-december-16th-2018-am-hope-for-the -holidays-(lk.-1:39–45).

If the object itself helps the audience understand, apply, or experience the text—if it advances the transformative point in the sermon—then, of course, use it. But what if it does not? What if it muddies the water like the juice and olive oil illustration does?

Another problem is that sometimes, instead of illustrating the point, an object simply represents an element of the text. Kelli Worrall provides the following example of how to use visuals to illustrate John 14:6:

> For example, if you are preaching from John 14 that Jesus is the way, the truth, and the life, you might use a prop to visualize each point. For "Jesus is the way," you might have a road sign. For the second point, "Jesus is the truth," you might reveal a carpenter's level. And when you articulate your third point, "Jesus is the life," you could uncover a thriving plant.[27]

While the visuals would provide a good representation of the word they are intended to illustrate, I'm not sure they do everything Worrall claims they will do: "These simple props would assist your congregation in focusing their attention, in understanding your message, and in remembering your outline for future growth and application." [28] I suspect they would do little to focus my attention, and more likely than not, they would be a distraction to me. Nor do I see how a street sign, a carpenter's level, or a healthy plant would help increase my understanding of this "I Am" statement from John's Gospel.

Professor Allan Moseley puts it well:

---

27. Worrall, "Drama and the Sermon," 304.
28. Worrall, "Drama and the Sermon," 304.

When some people think of illustrations, they think of object lessons, the kind ministers used commonly a few decades ago in "children's sermons." The idea behind such object lessons is that spiritual truth is difficult to understand, so we explain it with something that is visible and easy to understand. That makes sense, as far as it goes, but showing people a plant and talking about how God created plants does not show them how to worship the Creator. How much better to tell a story about someone who observed the creation, decided to worship God who created it all, and was completely changed by a relationship with the Creator.[29]

However, while I don't think the John 14:6 props would help members of the congregation focus their attention or understand the text, I suspect they could help make the text memorable, which is one of the strengths of object lessons—they are memorable. The stone and corn illustrations were memorable enough that I recall them twenty years later. Hart writes, "Visuals used prudently, selectively and with variation can not only enhance a homily, but help listeners to remember, recall and better understand the message."[30]

The key to Hart's observation is the prudent and selective use. One of the problems with the era around the turn of the millennium when preachers used props and visuals was the pressure to come up with an idea every week. The same thing happened when short video clips were popular. Every week, there was a pressure to find a funny video clip. With all the pressures of ministry, do we really want to add this one to the mix?

---

29. Moseley, *From the Study to the Pulpit*, 253.

30. Hart, "Creative Preaching," 94.

Conclusion:
Four Encouraging Words

The book began by examining four sermon illustration metaphors (bridge, window, light, and picture) and continued with four characteristics (familiar, clear, interesting, and appropriate) of effective illustrations. In conclusion, I want to leave you with four encouraging words.

Keep Illustrations in the Servant's Role

Sermon illustrations make wonderful servants but terrible masters. Illustrations serve.

Illustrations serve the **sermon**. Illustrations shouldn't just be memorable; they should make the sermon more memorable. Illustrations shouldn't just be interesting; they should stimulate interest in the sermon. We use them in service of the sermon.

Sermon illustrations serve the **text**. If we try to force a sermon illustration into a sermon where it doesn't quite fit—or if we use it to make ourselves look smart, creative, authentic, up-to-date, relevant, clever, etc.—we run the risk of our sermon illustration getting in the way of the text. And that is something we never want to do.

They serve the **listeners**. Ultimately, we use illustrations to serve the people. We find something that they are familiar with to help them understand, apply, or experience something that is foreign to them.

Keep Your Audience in Mind

Context matters. Make sure to consider the audience when selecting the illustration. An illustration might work well with one congregation but bomb with another one. There is no substitute for knowing the people you are preaching the gospel to. It isn't enough that you relate to the illustration; it must be relatable to the congregation.

With the advent of livestreaming, preachers must also consider the secondary audience that will be listening to the sermon. Some members of the secondary audience will be sympathetic to the mission of the church and the preacher's message; others will not. Be aware that there are some people who are "overhearing" your message. Take special care not to be offensive, either intentionally or inadvertently. None of us wants to erect barriers to the gospel; instead, we want to use our sermons and their illustrations to build bridges.

Use the Secondary Functions
of Each Illustration Type

Using a variety of sermon illustration types will not just curb predictability and stimulate greater interest in the sermon, but the variety will also help in the general faith development of the people. Each illustration type has a secondary function that can promote godliness.

Personal illustrations make preachers more relatable and help people connect with them. When you use them, be aware that your authentic, wholesome sharing of your life can have a catalytic effect on the spiritual growth of your hearers.

Fresh illustrations show how faith intersects with current culture. The relevance of the Bible emerges when you use current events, literature, or movies to help your audience understand, apply, or experience the text.

Biblical illustrations are the only authoritative sermon illustration type and expose the people to more of the whole counsel of God. It is God's word that will transform people's lives. Using biblical illustrations increases biblical literacy and adds depth and breadth to your preaching.

Hypothetical illustrations stimulate the imagination. Instead of limiting a text to a single application, they help the listeners see multiple ways that the text is significant and relevant to everyday life.

Historical illustrations provide a historical and theological context for contemporary faith practice. Without them, modern listeners can lose the valuable perspective of how the faithful before them lived, struggled, and found victory in Christ.

These secondary purposes should never be primary. In other words, the main reason we select an illustration is not because we want to self-disclose, show the intersection of faith and culture, or provide a historical or theological context for practicing the faith; the main reason we use illustrations is to help our listeners understand, apply, or experience the text. However, when we intentionally use the secondary purpose, we can promote spiritual growth and help develop our listeners in a holistic way.

Remember That You Are Still Preaching

Sermon illustrations are part of the sermon. Just as the sermon as a whole must communicate the message to the people, so must all of its component parts. Preachers need to be as careful, prayerful, and intentional in selecting their sermon illustrations as they are with biblical exegesis.

Effective sermon illustrations, when used well, help listeners understand, apply, or experience the text. However, they can also have the opposite effect. Poor illustrations can keep the listeners from hearing the message.

The thought that sermon illustrations can actually hinder people from hearing the message is a sobering reality. It is for this reason that we must illustrate well.

Bibliography

Adams, Jay E. *Preaching with Purpose*. Grand Rapids: Zondervan, 1981.

Akin, Daniel L. "Applying a Text-Driven Sermon." In *Text-Driven Preaching: God's Word at the Heart of Every Sermon*, edited by Daniel L. Akin, 269–94. Nashville: B&H Academic, 2010.

Akin, Daniel L., Bill Curtis, and Stephen Rummage. *Engaging Exposition: A 3-D Approach to Preaching*. Nashville: B&H Academic, 2011.

Allen, Jr., O. Wesley. *Determining the Form: Structures for Preaching*. Minneapolis: Augsburg Fortress, 2008.

Arnold, William V. "Protagonist Corner." *Journal for Preachers* 39, no. 2 (Lent 2016): 36.

Arthurs, Jeffrey. *Preaching with Variety: How to Re-Create the Dynamics of Biblical Genres*. Grand Rapids: Kregel, 2007.

Bailey, Raymond. "Ethics in Preaching." In *Handbook of Contemporary Preaching*, edited by Michael Duduit, 549–61. Nashville: Broadman, 1992.

Bergeson, Kevin D. "Sanctuary as Cinema?: Screens Should Not Block the Story." *Word & World* 32, no. 3 (Summer 2012): 303, 305.

Billings, Bradley S. "'As Some of Your Own Prophets Have Said':
Secular and Non-Canonical Literature in the New Testament
and Some Post-Modern Parallels." *The Expository Times* 123,
no. 10 (July 2012): 479–85.

Bisagno, John R. *Principle Preaching: How to Create and Deliver
Purpose Driven Sermons for Life Applications*. Nashville:
Broadman & Holman, 2002.

Blackwood, Andrew W. *Preaching from the Bible*. Grand Rapids:
Baker, 1977.

Blomberg, Craig L. *Preaching the Parables: From Responsible
Interpretation to Powerful Proclamation*. Grand Rapids: Baker
Academic, 2004.

Briscoe, Stuart. "The Subtle Temptations of Preaching." In *Mastering
Contemporary Preaching*, 141–52. Portland, OR: Multnomah,
1989.

Broadus, John Albert. *A Treatise on the Preparation and Delivery
of Sermons*. Edited by Edwin Charles Dargan. New York:
Hodder & Stoughton, 1898.

———. *Lectures on the History of Preaching*. New York: Sheldon &
Company, 1893.

Brown, David M. *Transformational Preaching: The Basics*. College
Station, TX: Vitualbookworm.com, 2010.

Brown, Jr., H. C. H., Gordon Clinard, Jesse J. Northcutt, and Al
Fasol. *Steps to the Sermon: An Eight-Step Plan for Preaching with
Confidence*. Revised. Nashville: Broadman & Holman, 1996.

Brown, Stephen. "Illustrating the Sermon." In *Handbook of
Contemporary Preaching*, edited by Michael Duduit, 199–208.
Nashville: Broadman, 1992.

Bush, George W. "Address to a Joint Session of Congress on Thursday Night, September 20, 2001." http://www.cnn.com/2001/US/09/20/gen.bush.transcript/.

Buttrick, David. *A Captive Voice*. Louisville: Westminster John Knox, 1994.

——. *Homiletic: Moves and Structures*. Philadelphia: Fortress, 1987.

Capill, Murray A. *Preaching with Spiritual Vigour: Including Lessons from the Life and Practice of Richard Baxter*. Geanies House, Scotland: Mentor, 2003.

Carter, Terry G., J. Scott Duvall, and J. Daniel Hays. *Preaching God's Word: A Hands-On Approach to Preparing, Developing, and Delivering the Sermon*. 2nd ed. Grand Rapids: Zondervan, 2018.

Chapell, Bryan. "Alternative Models." In *Handbook of Contemporary Preaching*, edited by Michael Duduit, 117–34. Nashville: Broadman, 1992.

——. *Christ-Centered Preaching: Redeeming the Expository Sermon*. 2nd ed. Grand Rapids: Baker Academic, 2005.

——. *Using Illustrations to Preach with Power*. Revised ed. Wheaton, IL: Crossway, 2001.

Charette, Vern. "Keeping Your People Glued to Jude: Using Illustrations that Stick." *Southwestern Journal of Theology* 58, no. 1 (Fall 2015): 43–51.

Chartier, Myron R. *Preaching as Communication: An Interpersonal Perspective*. Nashville: Abingdon, 1981.

Cornman, Thomas. "History: The Hidden Gold Mine." In *The Moody Handbook of Preaching*, edited by John Koessler, 251–66. Chicago: Moody, 2008.

Cox, James. "Evaluating the Sermon." In *Handbook of Contemporary Preaching*, edited by Michael Duduit, 225–35. Nashville: Broadman, 1992.

———. *Preaching: A Comprehensive Approach to the Design and Delivery of Sermons*. San Francisco: Harper & Row, 1985.

Craddock, Fred. *Preaching*. Nashville: Abingdon, 1985.

de Rosset, Rosalie. "Telling the Devil." In *The Moody Handbook of Preaching*, edited by John Koessler, 237–50. Chicago: Moody, 2008.

DeBrand, Roy. "The Visual in Preaching." In *Handbook of Contemporary Preaching*, edited by Michael Duduit, 398–408. Nashville: Broadman, 1992.

Deuel, David C. "Expository Preaching from Old Testament Narrative." In *Rediscovering Expository Preaching: Balancing the Science and Art of Biblical Exposition*, edited by John MacArthur, 273–87. Dallas: Word, 1992.

Easley, Michael. "Why Expository Preaching?" In *The Moody Handbook of Preaching*, edited by John Koessler, 27–38. Chicago: Moody, 2008.

Edwards, Jr., O. C. *Elements of Homiletic: A Method for Preparing to Preach*. Collegeville, MN: Liturgical Press, 1982.

Fabarez, Michael. *Preaching That Changes Lives*. Nashville: Thomas Nelson, 2002.

Fallon, Derrick T. "The Bible Preaches on the Bible: Transformation in Jesus' Proclamation." *Word & World* 32, no. 3 (Summer 2012): 294–301.

Farmer, Richard Allen. "What Sermon Illustrations Should Be Banned from Pulpits? Most of Them!" *Christianity Today* 58, no. 5 (June 2014): 31.

Feldman, Dana. "How Netflix is Changing the Future of Movie
        Theaters." *Forbes*, July 28, 2019. https://www.forbes.com/sites/
        danafeldman/2019/07/28/how-netflix-is-changing-the-future
        -of-movie-theaters/#1330d82b5f46.

Fleenor, Rob. "Samson the Judge: Critical Issues." In *The Lexham
        Bible Dictionary*, edited by John D. Barry. Bellingham, WA:
        Lexham Press, 2016.

Fuller, Charles. "Preaching and Education." In *Handbook of
        Contemporary Preaching*, edited by Michael Duduit, 464–73.
        Nashville: Broadman, 1992.

Galli, Mark. "Enough of Me Already!: It's Time to Find Other Ways
        to Illustrate Sermons than Me, Me, and Mine." *Leadership*
        31, no. 1 (Winter 2010). https://www.christianitytoday.com/
        pastors/2010/winter/enoughmeaready.html.

Galli, Mark, and Craig Brian Larson. *Preaching that Connects:
        Using Journalistic Techniques to Add Impact*. Grand Rapids:
        Zondervan, 1994.

Greear, J. D. "Pastor J.D., How Do You Prepare Your Sermons?" *J.D.
        Greear Blog*, December 8, 2015. https://jdgreear.com/pastor-j-d-
        how-do-you-prepare-your-sermons/

Greidanus, Sidney. *The Modern Preacher and the Ancient Text:
        Interpreting and Preaching Biblical Literature*. Grand Rapids:
        Eerdmans, 1988.

Hamilton, Donald L. *Homiletical Handbook*. Nashville: Broadman,
        1992.

———. *Preaching with Balance: Achieving and Maintaining Biblical
        Priorities in Preaching*. Geanies House, Scotland: Mentor, 2007.

Harbour, Brian L. "Concluding the Sermon." In *Handbook of
        Contemporary Preaching*, edited by Michael Duduit, 216–24.

Nashville: Broadman, 1992.

Hart, Richard. "Creative Preaching: Walk with Imagination in the Footsteps of Jesus." *The Priest* 68, no. 9 (September 2012): 89, 91–92, 94–95.

———. "Illustrations Enliven Our Preaching." *The Priest* 70, no. 3 (March 2014): 14, 16–18, 20–22, 24.

Hestenes, Roberta. "Not Everyone Learns Alike." In *Mastering Teaching, Mastering Ministry*. Portland, OR: Multnomah, 1991.

House, Paul. "Preaching in the Historical Books." In *Handbook of Contemporary Preaching*, edited by Michael Duduit, 280–94. Nashville: Broadman, 1992.

Huffman Jr., John A. "The Role of Preaching in Ministry." In *Handbook of Contemporary Preaching*, edited by Michael Duduit, 423–31. Nashville: Broadman, 1992.

Keller, Timothy. *Preaching: Communicating Faith in an Age of Skepticism*. New York: Penguin, 2016.

Krueger, Silas. "Preaching in an Oral Age: Preaching Styles That 'Speak' to a Post-Literate Generation." *Wisconsin Lutheran Quarterly* 122, no. 2 (Spring 2015): 83–125.

Lane, Adrian. "The God Who Illustrates: Using Illustrations in Preaching." *Churchman* 128, no. 4 (Winter 2014): 329–44.

Larsen, David L. *The Anatomy of Preaching: Identifying the Issues in Preaching Today*. Grand Rapids: Kregel, 1989.

Leonard, Bill J. "Preaching in Historical Perspective." In *Handbook of Contemporary Preaching*, edited by Michael Duduit, 21–33. Nashville: Broadman, 1992.

Lloyd-Jones, Martyn. *Preaching and Preachers*. Grand Rapids: Zondervan, 2011.

Lowry, Eugene L. *The Homiletical Plot: The Sermon as Narrative Art Form*. Louisville: Westminster John Knox, 2000.

MacArthur, John. "Rightly Dividing the Word of Truth: A Study Method for Faithful Preaching." In *Preach the Word: Essays on Expository Preaching*. Wheaton, IL: Crossway, 2007.

Mann, M. J. "Legends of Alexander." *The Second Achilles* (website), September 17, 2015. https://thesecondachilles.com/category/legends-of alexander/.

Mare, W. Harold. *New Testament Background Commentary: A New Dictionary of Words, Phrases and Situations in Bible Order*. Geanies House, Scotland: Mentor, 2004.

Mayhue, Richard L. "Introductions, Illustrations, and Conclusions." In *Rediscovering Expository Preaching*, 242–54. Dallas: Word, 1992.

McMickle, Marvin A. *Shaping the Claim: Moving from Text to Sermon*. Minneapolis: Augsburg Fortress, 2008.

Meet the Press, April 17, 1960. https://www.youtube.com/watch?v=1q88igiL_d8.

Merida, Tony. *Faithful Preaching: Declaring Scripture with Responsibility, Passion, and Authenticity*. Nashville: B&H Academic, 2009.

Miller, Calvin. *Preaching: The Art of Narrative Exposition*. Grand Rapids: Baker, 2006.

Miller, Kevin. "3 Questions to Ask When Preaching from Pop Culture: Avoid My Mistakes." *Anglican Compass* (blog), October 26, 2018. https://anglicancompass.com/3-questions -to-ask-when-preaching-from-pop-culture/.

Moseley, Allan. *From the Study to the Pulpit: An 8-Step Method for Preaching and Teaching the Old Testament*. Bellingham, WA: Lexham, 2017.

Moyer, J. C. "Samson." In vol. 3 of *The Zondervan Pictorial Encyclopedia of the Bible,* edited by Merrill C. Tenney. Grand Rapids: Zondervan, 1975.

Moyer, R. Larry. *Show Me How to Illustrate Evangelistic Sermons.* Show Me How series. Grand Rapids: Kregel Academic & Professional, 2012.

Nettles, Thomas J. "Charles Haddon Spurgeon: The Prince of Preachers." In vol. 2 of *A Legacy of Preaching,* edited by Benjamin K. Forrest, Kevin L. King, Bill Curtis, and Dwayne Milioni. Grand Rapids: Zondervan, 2018.

Palmer, Earl. "Preparing Yourself to Teach." In *Mastering Teaching, Mastering Ministry.* Portland, OR: Multnomah, 1991.

Patterson, Paige. "Ancient Rhetoric: A Model for Text-Driven Preachers." In *Text-Driven Preaching: God's Word at the Heart of Every Sermon*, edited by Daniel L. Akin, 11–36. Nashville: B&H Academic, 2010.

Price, Nelson. "Preaching and Church Growth." In *Handbook of Contemporary Preaching*, edited by Michael Duduit, 484–94. Nashville: Broadman, 1992.

Raiter, Michael. "On Sermons and Preaching 2: Preparing a Sermon." *St. Mark's Review* 219 (February 2012): 86–97.

Reinis, Austra. "*Exempla* in Sixteenth-Century Lutheran Sermons on Marriage Ethics." *Lutheran Quarterly* 27, no. 3 (Autumn 2013): 264–95.

Richard, Ramesh. *Scripture Sculpture: A Do-it-Yourself Manual for Biblical Preaching.* Grand Rapids: Baker, 1995.

Robinson, Haddon. *Biblical Preaching: The Development and Delivery of Expository Messages.* Grand Rapids: Baker Academic, 2014.

———. "Bringing Yourself into the Pulpit." In *Mastering Contemporary Preaching*, 127–40. Portland, OR: Multnomah, 1989.

———. *Making a Difference in Preaching: Haddon Robinson on Biblical Preaching*. Edited by Scott M. Gibson. Grand Rapids: Baker, 1999.

———. "Raisins in the Oatmeal: The Art of Illustrating." In *Preaching to Convince,* edited by James D. Berkley. Vol. 8 of *The Leadership Library*. Carol Stream, IL: Christianity Today; Waco, TX: Word, 1986.

———. "What Sermon Illustrations Should Be Banned from Pulpits? Any Story That's Just a Story." *Christianity Today* 58, no. 5 (June 2014): 31.

Sanlon, Peter. "Depth and Weight: Augustine's Sermon Illustration." *Churchman* 122, no. 1 (Spring 2008): 61–76.

Scharf, Greg. *Relational Preaching*. Cumbria, UK: Langham Preaching Resources, 2013.

Shaddix, Jim. *The Passion Driven Sermon: Changing the Way Pastors Preach and Congregations Listen*. Nashville: Broadman & Holman, 2003.

Sinibaldo, Geoff T. "Lousy Preaching and What to Do About It." *Lutheran Forum* 43, no. 1 (Spring 2009): 30–32.

Smith, Steven. "Stage Lights: Thoughts on Illustrating a Text." *Patheos Evangelical* (blog), April 6, 2011. https://www.patheos.com/resources/additional-resources/2011/04/stage-lights-thoughts-on-illustrating-a-text-steven-smith-04-07-2011.

Spurgeon, Charles H. *Lectures to My Students*. Third Series. Reprint, Grand Rapids: Baker, 1977.

Stanley, Andy and Lane Jones. *Communicating for a Change: Seven Keys to Irresistible Communication*. Portland, OR: Multnomah, 2006.

Stott, John R. W. *Between Two Worlds: The Challenge of Preaching Today*. Grand Rapids: Eerdmans, 1982.

Sunukjian, Donald. *Invitation to Biblical Preaching: Proclaiming Truth with Clarity and Relevance*. Grand Rapids: Kregel Academic, 2007.

Swindoll, Chuck. "Good Communication: Tell Me a Story." *The Pastor's Blog*, March 3, 2015. https://pastors.iflblog.com/2015/03/good-communication-tell-me-a-story/.

Thomas, Robert L. "Bible Translations and Expository Preaching." In *Rediscovering Expository Preaching: Balancing the Science and Art of Biblical Exposition*, edited by Richard L. Mayhue. Dallas: Word, 1992.

———. "Exegesis and Expository Preaching." In *Rediscovering Expository Preaching: Balancing the Science and Art of Biblical Exposition*, edited by Richard L. Mayhue. Dallas: Word, 1992.

Wiersbe, Warren W. and David Wiersbe. *The Elements of Preaching: The Art of Biblical Preaching Clearly and Simply Presented*. Wheaton, IL: Tyndale House, 1986.

Wilson, Jim L. *Future Church: Ministry in a Post-Seeker Age*. Nashville: Broadman & Holman, 2004.

Wilson, Jim L., and Earl Waggoner. *A Guide to Theological Reflection*. Grand Rapids: Zondervan Academic, 2020.

Wilson, Jim L., Gregg Watson, Michael Kuykendall, and David Johnson. *Impact Preaching: A Case for the One-Point Expository Sermon*. Bellingham, WA: Lexham, 2018.

Worrall, Kelli. "Drama and the Sermon." In *The Moody Handbook of Preaching*, edited by John Koessler, 293–308. Chicago: Moody, 2008.

York, Hershael W. and Bert Decker. *Preaching with Bold Assurance: A Solid and Enduring Approach to Engaging Exposition*. Nashville: Broadman & Holman, 2003.